THE HOME BAR

THE HOME BAR

A GUIDE TO DESIGNING, EQUIPPING AND STOCKING YOUR OWN BAR

PLUS OVER 30 RECIPES FOR COCKTAILS AND APERITIFS

HENRY JEFFREYS

FOREWORD BY ALEXANDRE RICARD

GIBBS SMITH
TO ENRICH AND INSPIRE HUMANKIND

First published in the United Kingdom in 2018 by
White Lion Publishing, part of the Quarto Group
The Old Brewery, 6 Blundell Street
London N7 9BH, United Kingdom
T (0)20 7700 6700 F (0)20 7700 8066
www.QuartoKnows.com

Published in the United States of America by
Gibbs Smith
P.O. Box 667
Layton, Utah 84041
1.800.835.4993 orders
www.gibbs-smith.com

Designed by White Lion Publishing

ISBN: 978-1-4236-4988-5
LCCN: 2018930029

21 20 19 18   5 4 3 2 1

Printed in China

A symphony in mirrored glass from American designers Haynes-Roberts, this bar reflects its stylish surrounding and its sheer scale makes the whisky bottles appear to be miniatures (*page 1*). Look closely and you will see recessed storage areas to the side for glasses.

You'd never think a gold-tiled bar could look this tasteful, but somehow interior designer Eric Hughes has pulled it off (*page 2*). But this New York duplex bar is no mere fashion accessory – with plenty of shelving, a built-in sink and a fridge, this is a serious piece of kit for the cocktail aficionado.

A bar that makes a feature of the beauty and variety of drink bottles (*this page*). Designed by Debra Parkington for a bar in a house in South Africa, it's all about minimalist lines that draw the eye towards the bottles backlit on glass shelves.

CONTENTS

Alexandre Ricard (right) with Daniel Gaujac, the project coordinator of his home bar.

WHEN I MOVED BACK TO PARIS five years ago after a long period abroad, I was tremendously excited about looking for a new apartment. Although I have to say I was most excited by the idea of finally having my own home bar—finding the ideal space to house it was my number one priority while I was flat hunting! I even had a name for it before it was built. It would be *Le bar des amis*, a place for my friends to hang out and the focus of my home. To be honest, I'm still not sure if the bar is in my living room or if the living room is around the bar…

I am a grandson of Paul Ricard, the man who invented the most popular French aperitif that bears our family name. I wouldn't go as far as saying I was brought up around bars, but every time we visited my uncles and aunts, they all had their own home bars. Some people have a *Sex in the City* style closet for their shoe collection, or a huge garage for their fancy cars; we had home bars.

My grandfather started the home bar tradition by building one in his home, *La Tête de l'Évêque* in Provence, located on a mountainside overlooking the Formula 1 racing circuit that bears his name. It was a modest bar with long wooden shelves displaying 40 or so spirits around a mirror, that occupied half of the living room. Thirty years after he passed away, his bar is still intact. I keep a blurry picture in my wallet of the two of us standing there, glasses in hand. The bottles in that picture are still there today, untouched since 1997. As a family, whenever we visit the house, we don't touch Papy's bottles, but always open a new bottle of Ricard.

Pernod Ricard, which my grandfather co-founded, is now the world's number two in wines and spirits. There's a good chance that most of your bars, big or small, feature at least some of our 350 brands. Our Group's signature is "*Créateurs de Convivialité*," to represent the genuine pleasure of sharing a moment of celebration and togetherness with friends and family. And a bar should be the place that inspires that spirit of *convivialité*.

My home bar is semi-circular in shape, to make it more convivial and easier to mingle. Its marble base rests on a floor of virgin oak and is decorated with the Ricard logo in the form of a sunburst. The zinc counter is typical of most French bars, but the rim is studded with a beading of star anise and carries my grandfather's slogan, written in his own hand: *Faites-vous un ami par jour*, or Make a new friend every day.

The stuff home bar dreams are made of—Alexandre Ricard's Paris apartment (**opposite**). This semi-circular 1930s-style bar is the work of a pair of master craftsmen from L'Etainier Tourangeau.

I have more than 600 bottles at home, all of them from our own family of brands. Some stand behind the bar, others cover the walls; I enjoy seeing my visitors stare at them as if they were in an art gallery. The difference is that these pieces are made to be touched and tasted.

The look of my bar changes constantly; it's very fluid. I like to refresh it on a regular basis, move bottles around and change the focus of the back bar depending on my mood. It's a great relaxation tool!

When I'm in Paris, I enjoy entertaining at home. Apéritifs are served at the bar and we generally offer the starter there too. The main course and dessert will be eaten at the dining table and then we will all gravitate back to the bar for coffee, tea, and digestifs—it's less formal and more sociable.

I always encourage my friends to move around the bar, to spend time in front as well as behind, and to mix their own drinks. The whole experience of mixing contributes to the convivial atmosphere. Making cocktails is fun, especially when you dare to unleash your creativity and play around by adding your own personal twists to traditional recipes.

Not a single day goes by when having a bar in my home does not lift my spirits. Even when the room is quiet and empty, it feels as if it's just waiting—ready and eager to host another moment of *convivialité*. It makes me want to ask the favorite question of every happy owner of a home bar: "What can I get you to drink?"

On the zinc-topped counter, a gorgeous stepped Art Deco champagne flute sits alongside some pretty high-grade cocktailing kit, including a Hawthorne strainer and a squat shaker (*opposite, top left*).

A look behind Alexandre Ricard's home bar; many professional bartenders would give their eye teeth for a set-up like this (*opposite, top right*). Note the enormous cold tray for ice, the sink, and the sunken chilled compartment to store garnishes.

This bookshelf in Alexandre Ricard's apartment hosts a collection of antique shakers (*opposite, below*). The photograph by Eric Morin shows a detail of the zinc counter of the bar with a quote in Ricard's grandfather's hand.

The bar occupies an entire wall of the living room (*overleaf*). Designed by Gaétan Lebègue, the seating area features a coffee table by Stefan Nikolaev—a tongue-in-cheek giant replica of the classic yellow Opalex glass Ricard ashtray of the 1960s.

THE EVOLUTION OF THE HOME BAR

The growing global popularity of iced cocktails such as the Dry Martini in bars led to people wanting to recreate the experience in the comfort of their own homes. Initially cocktail parties were just for the rich, but during the post-war period a fully stocked home bar became part of the suburban dream all over the world.

This mahogany cocktail cabinet was originally a military chest, but has been remodeled for bibulous purposes by American designer Ken Fulk (*opposite*). To prevent pilfering, the precious contents are guarded by a suitably military-looking penguin.

A HISTORY OF DRINKING

What could be more hospitable than a properly made drink? Not just a gin and tonic or whisky and soda, but what about whipping your guests up a Daiquiri, a Martini or a Brooklyn? Furthermore, rather than scrabbling around in the cupboard, wouldn't it be wonderful if all the ingredients were laid out for easy use, and there was a plentiful supply of ice and the right glasses? If you're thinking along these lines then this book is for you. You can start small, perhaps just a tray, a shaker, and an ice bucket or a small cart, but be warned: you might soon be hankering after something with a zinc top, bar stools, and a built-in sound system.

But we're getting ahead of ourselves; before the home bar, there was the public bar. It might surprise you to learn that the bar as such, a counter from which drinks are served, is a relatively recent invention. Prior to the early 19th century, an alehouse or tavern would not be far removed from a private house—you were a guest of the landlord and one of his many daughters would bring you your drink. You might have to wait for some time, but then you probably weren't in a hurry. In contrast, the bar was a production line for drinking. One could serve an enormous number of customers quickly. What the steam locomotive was to travel and the power loom was to weaving, the bar was to drinking.

The drink itself was becoming industrialized, too. At these new-fangled bars, the beer would have come from vast commercial brewers such as Whitbread in London or Guinness in Dublin, rather than on the premises, brewed by the landlord's wife. Gin, too, was going high tech: in 1830 Dubliner

Aeneas Coffey patented a new kind of still which meant that a spirit of great purity could be produced safely and efficiently. It meant an end to the sort of dodgy gin that might poison you. From the 1830s private companies built elaborate "gin palaces." They employed well-known designers such as John Buonarotti Papworth, who did the interior of gentlemen's club Boodle's. These places with their polished wood, etched glass, and gas lamps provided cheap glamour and a warm refuge from the freezing London winter. They were the Art Deco movie theaters of their time.

Whereas poorer sorts went to gaudy gin palaces, the middle classes were turning inwards. Houses were becoming snugger, with carpets, better windows and more efficiently designed heating systems. From the 1850s entertaining at home was the in thing and people picked up the new-fangled French habit of offering a drink before the meal, rather than just binging on port at the end. As well as port, a fairly affluent family might offer their guests sherry or, if they were really fancy, champagne and spirits such as whisky, cognac and gin. Valuable drinks needed to be kept safe from untrustworthy servants or prying children, so people bought drinks cabinets or lockable decanters. These elaborate contraptions built of hardwood and brass with secret compartments were early prototypes of the home bar.

The Cocktail Bar at the Penna D'Oca Restaurant in Milan. It was designed by Tomaso Buzzi, Emilio Lancia, Michele Marelli, and Gio Ponti around 1928 (*opposite*). They were part of a group of innovative designers and architects based in Milan who blended classical architecture and traditional craftsmanship with Art Deco.

Outside the home, drinks were becoming increasingly elaborate. A city pub might knock you up a Gloom Lifter, an Eye Opener, a Morning Jolt and, for when all else fails, a Corpse Reviver. These were a genre of drinks known as antifogmatic, designed to keep out London's infamous cold. American cocktails were more jolly (the first description of a "cocktail" came in 1806 from New York paper *The Balance and Columbian Repository*). Charles Dickens on his American book tour was amazed by the ubiquity of iced drinks like Mint Juleps, Sherry Cobblers, and chilled punches. Ice was a rare luxury in Europe, but commonplace in America. They would harvest ice in the winter and store it in special ice boxes, forerunners of modern refrigerators and chiller compartments.

It was the start of something like a modern cocktail culture. Recipes were being codified by men such as Jerry Thomas, head bartender at the Eldorado Hotel in San Francisco in his bestselling book *The Classic Guide to Cocktails* (1887). One such recipe was for a sweet gin-based cocktail called the Martinez, which is thought to be the forerunner of the Dry Martini. Nobody quite knows the origin of the name, but that mixture of London dry gin, French vermouth (wine fortified and flavored) and, of course, ice would prove iconic.

Thomas toured Europe spreading the cocktail gospel. Bars selling American-style (that is, iced) cocktails opened in big cities around the world, in London, Paris, Shanghai, and Buenos Aires. Advances in refrigeration meant ice could be made in situ rather than having to be shipped in from America—they really used to haul huge blocks of ice across the Atlantic. Not everyone was impressed. According to literary critic and wine writer Robert Saintsbury it was a "barbarous time" when vulgar people even started drinking their claret chilled.

Cocktails were just part of the post-World War I craze for all things American, like jazz music, enormous cars, milk bars, and motion pictures. American movies promised glamour, sexual liberation, and consumerism. Life began to imitate art: the Art Deco Strand Palace Hotel in London looked like a film set, not surprising as it was designed by Oliver Bernard, who had been a set designer in Hollywood (the foyer is now in the Victoria & Albert Museum in London).

The great thing about having people over for cocktails is that it didn't require the work or expense of a dinner party. All you needed was booze, ice, glasses, and some basic equipment. They proved particularly popular in England as there was a shortage of servants following the war—one simply could not get the staff. The novelist Alec Waugh claimed to have introduced them to London in 1924, a boast his brother, Evelyn Waugh, was quick to scoff at. No matter who invented it, the cocktail hour between 5 and 7pm quickly took off among the bright young things.

In the '20s, Harry MacElhone, a Scot who had tended bar in New York, opened Harry's Bar in Paris and Harry Craddock, an Englishman from New York's Knickerbocker Hotel, opened the American Bar at the Savoy Hotel in London. Both Harrys had been chased out of the US by Prohibition, which became law in January 1920. It was the death of the saloon bar, but boom time for the home bar because although it was illegal to make and sell alcohol, you were allowed to drink in

A shot of the decidedly non-minimalist back bar at Harry's New York Bar in Paris (**opposite**). Founded in 1911, it was the haunt of Ernest Hemingway, Gertrude Stein, and F. Scott Fitzgerald, and where bartender extraordinaire Harry MacElhone created such immortal cocktails as the Bloody Mary and the Sidecar.

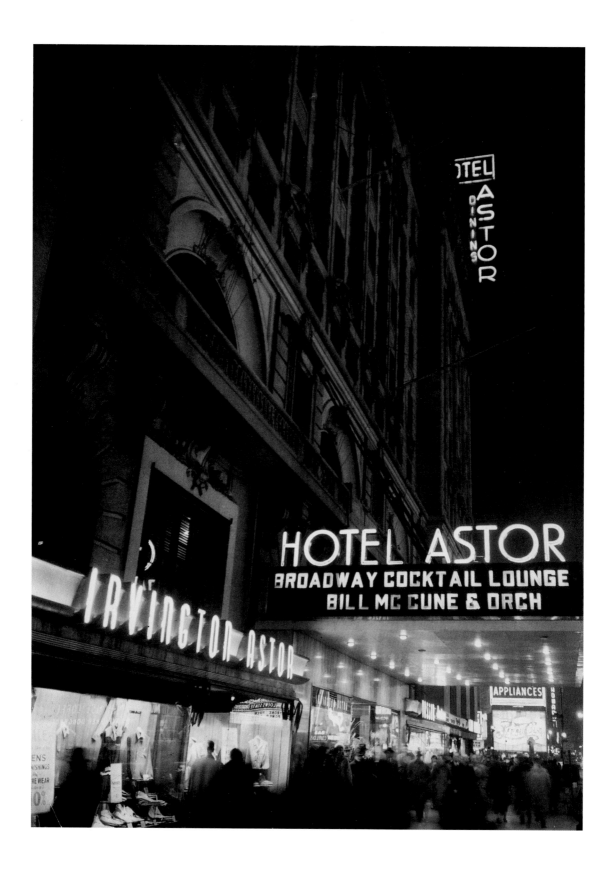

A view of the Hotel Astor in 1955 (*opposite*). It was built in a Parisian Beaux-Arts style near Times Square between 1905 and 1910, and quickly became one of the most fashionable venues in town. Sadly, this icon of New York glamour was demolished in 1967 to make way for a skyscraper.

Looking like a chemist measuring out an antidote, this is actually Harry Craddock at the American Bar of the Savoy Hotel in London in 1926 (*above*). An Englishman by birth, he was the man responsible for introducing American-style cocktails such as the Dry Martini to Europe.

The Milk Bar in Bear Street, London circa 1936 (*above*). Milk bars selling exotic drinks such as "milkshakes" were part of the pre-war mania for all things American. They arrived in the '30s just after the cocktail bar, but disappeared during World War II when milk was rationed.

a private house or club. At home elaborate Art Deco cabinets were available to serve your drinks from. Philco, an American radio company, offered a radio that opened up into a cocktail cabinet. It featured in the gangster flick *Angels with Dirty Faces* (1938) starring James Cagney and Humphrey Bogart. You could order your Philco in a traditional wood veneer or in modern materials such as chromium, aluminum, and Bakelite. The top-of-the-range models cost as much as a new luxury car.

But unless you were a member of the Yale Club, who on the eve of Prohibition bought up enough booze for its members to last 14 years, then obtaining alcohol wasn't straightforward. You could either pay through the nose for drinks smuggled in from Canada or Bermuda, or you would do as most people did and drink so-called bathtub alcohol: industrial alcohol flavored or colored to taste and look—not very much—like gin, whisky, bourbon, etc. Your gin might be adulterated with sulphuric acid. Mmm, tangy! You wouldn't want to drink that in a Dry Martini, so during Prohibition cocktails became sweeter and fruitier to disguise the taste of the bad liquor. Al Capone's favorite cocktail was a Southside, a mixture of gin, lemon, sugar, and mint. Another popular '20s cocktail was the Bronx, made with orange juice, sweet vermouth, and gin. For those who didn't want to drink at home, there were speakeasies (see page 48), illegal bars that could range from someone's living room to elaborate nightclubs in Harlem. White people would go uptown to drink. According to a columnist in a New York paper: "the night clubs have done more to improve race relations in ten years than the churches, white and black, have in ten decades." And in contrast to the all-male saloon bars of old, speakeasies welcomed women. The spirit of the free-drinking modern female was captured in the 1929 silent film *Our Modern Maidens* starring Joan Crawford, which featured the immortal line "Lunch is poured." When Prohibition was finally repealed in 1933, the drinking culture had been utterly transformed, alcohol for women had been normalized, and spirits were king. This set the pattern for home drinking until the 1960s.

After World War II, the US, in particular, boomed, and people moved away from the inner cities, with their bars and nightclubs, and into the suburbs. People were spending more time in their homes, but they still wanted to lead the cocktail lifestyle: you could listen to Frank Sinatra's *Songs for Swingin' Lovers!* (1956) on your state of the art hifi, and no self-respecting American home would be without at least a drinks tray, more probably a cocktail cart or even a built-in home bar.

It was the American male dream: a family, a new car every couple of years, a big house in the suburbs, and an ice-cold Martini or two when you came home from work. This heyday of the home bar was reflected in the culture of the times. In Richard Yates's alcohol-soaked novel *Revolutionary Road* (1961), the hero, Frank Wheeler, daydreams about "a white wrought-iron table set with ice and cocktail mixings." With the return of quality booze, the cocktail, the Martini especially, was elevated into an art form. The poet laureate of post-war cocktail culture was Bernard DeVoto. In his 1949 book *The Hour* he came up with the immortal dictum on the importance of making your drink fresh every time: "You can no more keep a Martini in the refrigerator than you can keep a kiss there."

The look moved on from the Art Deco of the 1920s and '30s, to modernism in the '40s and '50s. In 1951 came the Festival of Britain, which was meant to be a celebration of British design and the optimism of the postwar period, but architectural critic Jonathan Meades refers to it as the Festival of Scandinavia, such was the influence of North Eurporean design. This impact was felt internationally. The era of chic minimalist design and strong liquor will be familiar to viewers of *Mad Men*, a series that went to great lengths to get the details in dress, furniture, and, of course, alcohol absolutely right.

But it wasn't all Nordic good taste. As the '50s gave way to the '60s, stripped-back minimalism was out and interior design became more riotous. We can see the change from a movie like *High Society* (1956) in which Frank Sinatra, Bing Crosby, and Grace Kelly booze and croon around an understated mid-century bar, to Anne Bancroft trying to seduce Dustin Hoffman in *The Graduate* (1967) at a kitsch home bar complete with tiki-style glasses and a big glowing sign saying "Bar," presumably in case drunk guests forgot where they were.

From this point on the home bar lost its cool, though not its popularity. It was mocked in movies such as 1978's *Foul Play*, in which Dudley Moore plays a swinger who tries to seduce Goldie Hawn with a piano that turns into a (let's face it, completely fabulous) bar. The cocktail was becoming a bit of a joke.

By the 1980s stricter drunk driving laws led to the end of the suburban boozing lifestyle. The home bar seemed an anachronism, as did spending time making cocktails. Wine consumption was rocketing in English-speaking countries. Now when you went to someone's house you'd be offered the choice of

Art Deco heaven (*opposite, top*). This photograph showing two white-liveried bartenders standing ready to serve in a circular bar is from around 1935. Look at those beautiful bar stools!

This bar is actually from around 1958 but it looks like it has been beamed in from the future (*opposite, below*). I particularly like the way the bottles are displayed behind circular windows, in classic space-age design.

Not even Soviet Russia was immune to the lure of the cocktail (*right*). This photograph was taken at a majestic cocktail bar in Gorky Street in Moscow in 1941. The street was named after the writer Maxim Gorky, a great champion of the Party. It reverted back to its pre-revolutionary name of Tverskaya Street in 1990.

Join the mile-high club (*below*). Known as the "flying cocktail lounge," this is the bar inside Howard Hughes's Boeing 307 Stratoliner, the world's first aircraft with a pressurized cabin. Because of its plush interior, it could accommodate only 16 (extremely lucky) people.

red or white wine. That great lover of spirits and author Kingsley Amis wrote that the most depressing words when meeting a friend for lunch were: "Shall we go straight in?" closely followed by "red or white?" It was the time when the word "gentrification" was coined. In the US and Britain, the middle classes were moving back to the inner cities into old Victorian houses. It was the era of the informal dinner party, but generally people were entertaining less at home and going out more. Eating out was the thing. As Bruno Kirby's character in *When Harry Met Sally* (1989) put it: "Restaurants are to people in the '80s what theater was to people in the '60s."

Many home bars were scrapped or relegated to the garage, rather than being the centerpoint of the room. Home bar became synonymous with the dreaded "man cave"—which for me misses the point of cocktails: they are meant to be unisex. The home bar was down, but it was not out. In the '90s there was a reappraisal of '50s suburban culture. A young crowd rediscovered the joys of easy listening, suits, and cocktail dresses. People could pick up home bars for a song at garage sales or they would buy or rent houses that had them built in. The Seattle-based DJ and cocktail aficionado Terence Gunn has written of how there was a brief vogue in the States for home bar crawls. Those Formica-topped bars from the 1970s are now collectors' items.

Meanwhile the cocktail itself was being reinvigorated by bartenders such as Dick Bradsell at the Atlantic Bar in London, inventor of the Espresso Martini and the Bramble, and Dale DeGroff at the Rainbow Room in New York. A new generation were discovering the joy of Art Deco hotels like Claridge's in London and the classic cocktails from the golden era, the

Manhattan, the Negroni, and, of course, the Martini. Nowadays, there's a wide palate of flavors to choose from. Small distilleries have opened all over the world, and the choice of gins, whiskies, vermouths, and brandies is now better than ever. People, both professional and amateur, are experimenting with making their own infusions, flavored vodkas, vermouth, and syrups, and aging cocktails for a more complex taste.

So if you're seriously interested in cocktails then you need somewhere to keep all the equipment, bottles, and glasses. But a home bar isn't really about practicality, it's about showing off. It's about entertaining, it's about pretending that you are Humphrey Bogart or Joan Crawford for the evening. Whether you've got a drinks alcove or custom-made bar in your warehouse apartment, invite your friends over, get your shaker out, and let your imagination run wild. This book will provide a little inspiration, but the rest is up to you.

Bottles and decanters stand ready on a dome-topped metal and glass shelving unit (**opposite**). It makes an elegant counterpoint to its backdrop, a collaboration between American designer Ken Fulk and wallpaper company de Gournay, entitled "Madame's Magical Menagerie." Everything is hand-painted.

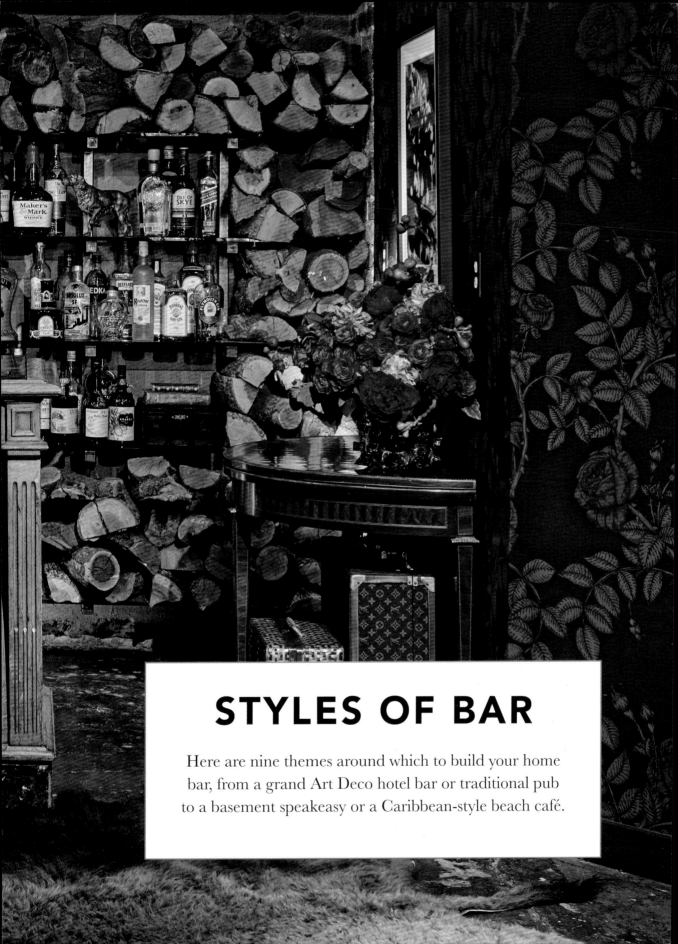

STYLES OF BAR

Here are nine themes around which to build your home bar, from a grand Art Deco hotel bar or traditional pub to a basement speakeasy or a Caribbean-style beach café.

This chapter looks at how to recreate a classic or contemporary bar in your own home, with tips on everything from art to put on the walls to the right kind of music to get you in the mood.

This is a bar in a private home designed by Ken Fulk, mixing wood, brick and worn leather for that log cabin meets gentleman's club look (*previous pages*). The bottles are surrounded by split logs for the wood-burning stove.

From *House & Garden* magazine in 1933, this portable bar murmurs tasteful Art Deco glamour with its black linoleum top and aluminum sides polished to produce a striped effect (*opposite*). The matching striped Martini glasses are a nice touch.

GRAND HOTELS AND CAFES

Art Deco hotels are the golden age of cinema in steel and concrete. A Martini or two at the bar in Claridge's in London and for an hour you could be Greta Garbo in *Grand Hotel* (1932) or Fred Astaire in *Top Hat* (1935)—just don't try to dance like him. The movies fed off industrial design and vice versa: Michel Dufet, who designed the first-class staterooms for the 1935 ocean liner the *Normandie*, also built sets for the film industry. The Art Deco look was inspired by new technology such as passenger aircraft, aerodynamic automobiles, high-speed trains, and vast new ocean-going liners. Which is why your cocktail cabinet might have the aerodynamic lines of a Bugatti coupé, when all it did was sit there waiting for you to make a drink. It was all about speed, modernity, and novelty.

Cities were built in an Art Deco style: think of the Chrysler Building or Radio City Music Hall in New York. The downtowns of major American cities are Art Deco wonderlands (though often in a shocking state of disrepair). The name Art Deco comes from the 1925 Exposition Internationale des Arts Décoratifs et Industriels Modernes in Paris, but the style is older. It emerged in France just before World War I and was an offshoot of, or perhaps a reaction to, Art Nouveau—the grand *fin de siècle* style. The difference between the two styles,

This mural by Alfred R. Thompson showing a London carnival scene features in the bar of the *Queen Mary* (*left*). When it was launched in 1936, this ocean liner was the last word in Art Deco luxury. It steamed on until 1967, when it was retired by the Cunard Line.

One of New York City's best-kept secrets is the Campbell Apartment Cocktail Bar, tucked away in a corner of Grand Central Station (*opposite, top*). With its fabulously ornate ceiling, leaded windows, and enormous fireplace, the bar has something of a medieval feel.

Another Alfred R Thompson mural, *Jubilee Week*, is in the Observation Bar on the *Queen Mary* (*opposite, below*). The liner is now a floating hotel in Long Beach, California.

Plum + Spilt Milk, the dining room inside the Great Northern Hotel near King's Cross Station in London, is inspired by the golden age of railway travel (*above*). It is named after the distinctive livery of the dining cars on the Flying Scotsman, once the world's fastest train.

An elegant way to get a bit of big hotel grandeur in a domestic setting (*left*). This curved and polished wooden bar, with shiny chrome and leather bar stools, has a distinctly Art Deco feel.

wood veneers—which is how it began in France— or a mass-produced style providing cheap glamour in Bakelite, chrome, and mirrored glass for movie-goers. For the young, Art Deco was something their parents might disapprove of, along with jazz music, racy cinema, and female emancipation.

After many years of neglect, the Art Deco look is now revered. The great hotel bars that were beginning to look a little shabby have been returned to their pre-war splendor. Claridge's Hotel was refurbished in the '90s and the American Bar at the Savoy reopened in 2010 following three years of refurbishment. Over in New York, the magnificent Oyster Bar at Grand Central Station was restored to its former glory in 2014. Now new venues often go for the grand Deco look: interior designer Martin Brudnizki has brought pre-war glamour back to London's dining scene with his work for the Ivy restaurant chain and the revamped restaurant in Fortnum & Mason in Piccadilly.

according to the writer Bevis Hillier, was that Art Deco was "rectilinear not curvilinear." Deco, as the name suggests, was a decorative style, with graphic motifs like stepped profiles, chevrons, and zigzags appearing on often quite plain pieces.

From there though it is difficult to generalize about what Art Deco was, as it absorbed exotic influences from Japan, pre-Columbus America and in particular ancient Egypt, following the discovery of Tutankhamun's tomb in 1922. Deco could be both a high-art luxury style made by craftsmen in luxury

So where does this leave the home bar enthusiast who doesn't have the services of a top-end interior designer? The good news is that Deco can work on a small scale. Nothing says 1930s quite like a traditional cocktail shaker and Martini glass on a plain silver tray. Particularly in big cities like London and New York, bright young things might have a small deco apartment in a new mansion block. Companies such as Epstein in London offer drink cabinets in lavish wood veneers. Once you've found your perfect bar, you could go for the complete Bertie Wooster's bachelor flat look. It doesn't all need to be original: a couple of good pieces and some reproduction would work well. Look for creams and blacks and pieces with polished wood veneers, Bakelite, and lots of chrome. A big rug with a geometric design on bare floorboards would complete the look.

But rather than try to imitate the high Art Deco style of Claridge's or Hollywood, instead take your inspiration from the interwar French café with its zinc-topped bar. You can buy or build a plain bar and have it topped with zinc, and then decorate your room with jazz posters featuring Josephine Baker, classic '20s drinks advertisements for Sandeman Port, or motor racing posters from French illustrator Geo Ham. Add a few well-chosen lamps, a glass of Ricard, and a carafe of iced water, and your home bar will quickly feel like a hotspot in '20s Montmartre. Remember that Deco is meant to be fun, frivolous, and sexy, and you can't go wrong.

A zinc top will lend your home bar a certain *je ne sais quoi* (*right*). This surface, found in traditional French bistros, not only looks gorgeous but it is extremely practical as it doesn't need polishing, unlike wood or copper.

Despite being in a brand-new 49-story apartment building, the Harrison in San Francisco, this green-paneled bar designed by Ken Fulk has an intimate feel that would not look out of place in the home (*overleaf*). And with bar stools like those, you'll never want to leave.

The poster is by Felix Vallotton for Byrrh, a wine-based quinine-flavored aperitif (*above*). On the table is a glass of Suze "on the rocks," another bitter French drink, with a 1950s Suze bottle.

You don't need a big room for a home bar, as this retro-style wooden bar by interior designers Turner Pocock shows (*above*). This would work in a city apartment, especially with mid-century-inspired stools.

THE CLASSIC BAR

Like Christmas, the urban bar or pub as we know it, all dark mahogany, brass fittings, and mirrored glass, is essentially a Victorian invention. Prior to the 19th century you would have had three categories of places to drink: alehouses which only sold beer, and might just be a room in somebody's house, taverns, which had many rooms and generally sold wine rather than beer to the better off, and inns, which were for travelers and functioned like hotels. From around the 1820s things began to change, when new public houses were built, often at great expense, or old ones were renovated. The most elaborate pubs were known as "gin palaces" because they were so ornate. Thomas Hardy's 1895 novel *Jude the Obscure* captures the spirit of the times (it was set in the mid 19th century): "the bar had been gutted and newly arranged throughout, mahogany fixtures having taken the place of the old painted ones . . ."

That classic pub look—familiar to the British and Irish and seen in a few surviving versions on the east coast of America—far from being traditional and old-fashioned would have seemed gaudy and strange to early Victorians. This is an important thing to remember when trying to recreate a pub at home. If you buy a new mahogany (or a faux mahogany) bar, it's not going to look like the one in your favorite boozer that might have had nearly 200 years of use. Furthermore, you are unlikely to find something with the sheer craftsmanship that went into those old pubs. New home bars in a traditional style tend to look a bit reproduction, but then again so do some pubs—many were refitted in the '60s in a "traditional" style. If you are buying a brand-new pub bar or having one made, look for

something plain and ideally in solid mahogany—chipboard with a veneer won't look right.

If you have a big enough room you could go hunting for an original 19th-century bar in salvage yards or online. For a smaller space, antique drug store counters make a good alternative, though they do lack the storage space. Unless your room is enormous, it's probably better to err on the side of caution when buying a bar: too big and it will dominate the room. Ideally the bar will come with a mirrored back bar where you can display your bottles, but if not you could always use an old hutch or something similar and pretend that you're going for the country pub look.

If you're going to be doing a lot of entertaining, it might be worth investing in the taps, plumbing, gas, cooling, and of course the keg required for draught beer. It will need regular maintenance and cleaning, so if you don't think you're going to drink that much beer, a good choice of bottled beer will be fine.

With your bar in place, it's time to build your pub look around it. The best way to do this is to spend some time in your favorite bar. You can pretend it's research. Classic gin palaces that are worth visiting include the Red Lion on Jermyn Street and the Princess Louise in Holborn, London. Or

The amazing gin palace-style interior of the Princess Louise in Holborn, London is a riot of mirrors and carved wood (**opposite**). It was designed by William B. Simpson & Sons, and dates back to 1891, but was fully restored by the current owners, Yorkshire-based Samuel Smith Brewery, in 2007.

in New York marvel at one of the last surviving
19th-century pubs, the Old Town Bar on 18th
Street with its enormously long bar and tiled floor.
When conducting your research look at your
surroundings: is there a lot of bric-a-brac? Is there
a carpet, wooden floorboards or flagstones? How
dark is it and how is it lit? Are those signs saying
"You don't have to be mad to work here" or "Free
beer tomorrow" really necessary?

Old bars tend to be palimpsests, with layers of
change written over Victorian or older foundations.
This means that the look is very adaptable. You
can build a gentlemen's club around your bar,
with leather armchairs, bookshelves, and a liveried
manservant called Jenkins. You can make it look
more rural, with hunting prints and agricultural

Thanks to Prohibition, there are very few 19th-century
saloon bars left in America. A rare survivor is the Old
Town Bar near Union Square in New York, with its marble
and mahogany bar, distressed mirrors and authentic
pressed tin ceiling (*above*).

You're bound to get thirsty after all that reading; every
library in the country should have a bar as well-stocked
as this one at Badminton House in Gloucestershire
(*opposite*). Note the portrait of the Marquess of Bath
by Graham Sutherland guarding the drinks.

paraphernalia. Games are always welcome, such as a dart board, a bar billiards table, or, for a more modern take, perhaps an original Space Invaders table. Or, you could go for the downtown bar look, with neon beer signs, a pool table, and a pinball machine—even a jukebox.

The best thing about the traditional pub look is once you've splashed out on the bar—and it is worth spending some money on getting a good solid bar—then the rest of the stuff, old family photos, brewery signs, taxidermy, maps etc. can generally be picked up extremely cheaply. To most people this is just junk, but somehow it looks right in a pub. And if all else fails, dim lighting will cover a multitude of sins.

A wood-paneled bar in a Georgian house devised by interior designer Mark Gillette (*below*). From the country pursuit paintings to the fire seats, the style is full-on gentleman's club. The bottles on the bar are discreetly lit to provide a focus for the room. Brandy and soda anyone?

You can mix styles as long as you do it with confidence, as in this set-up (*opposite*): the bar is Arts and Crafts, the rug and the striped wallpaper have an Art Deco look, the armchairs could have come from a St James's club and it is all finished off with playfully kitsch cushions.

A compact corner cocktail bar in the living room of a New York apartment designed Bibi Monnahan (*opposite*). The look is '50s Hollywood glamour with the lipstick-hued paint, red roses, and matching velvet chair. Eagle-eyed readers will note the photo of Sophia Loren looking disapprovingly at Jayne Mansfield's cleavage.

URBAN SPEAKEASY

When Prohibition began on January 16, 1920 and the saloons closed for good, a whole host of private operations sprang up to replace them. Selling alcohol may have become illegal, but most people still wanted a drink. Official estimates put the number at between 20,000 and 100,000 places illegally selling alcohol in New York City alone. Some might be Italian restaurants offering you something a little stronger than Coca-Cola with your pasta, or back rooms in barber shops, or the enormous hidden nightclubs celebrated in films like *The Roaring Twenties* (1939), *Once Upon a Time in America* (1984), and mostly luridly Baz Luhrmann's *The Great Gatsby* (2013), but most speakeasies would be simpler, temporary affairs. There was no point investing in expensive fixtures or even a proper bar when the cops might bust you at any moment and shut you down. Where you served your drinks from might be a makeshift affair made from packing cases, tea chests, or trunks. In this way the speakeasy might be the ultimate home bar look, because most speakeasies were just that: bars in someone's home.

This makes the urban speakeasy one of the easiest and cheapest looks to attain when creating your home bar. The internet is full of guidelines for how to make a bar out of wooden pallets or similar. It could even be something as simple as an old door propped up on wooden or metal filing cabinets. Wooden wine boxes can serve many purposes: as footstools, drawers, or screwed to the walls as shelves. Speakeasies would often be in back rooms, warehouses, and basements, so exposed brickwork looks good, as do metal beams and bare lightbulbs. You don't want too much natural light getting in. If you are thinking of a '20s and '30s industrial look, with old-fashioned radiators, air ducts, and heavy copper pipes (perhaps secretly carrying bootleg whisky) then you're on the right track. Victorian tiles would be superb, or you could invest in a pressed-tin ceiling. For the walls, try a grand old mirror with plenty of tarnish and, though not a particularly authentic look, '20s/'30s movie posters would give your illicit drinking den a good feel.

Speakeasy-style bars are everywhere. But for the authentic feel you have to have some law-breaking on the premises. This 1920s Chicago speakeasy bar is where Ben Yount was found murdered (**left**).

Hard to believe that this breathtaking bar in the Pernod Distillery at Thuir in southern France was once the typing pool (**opposite**). The conversion makes full use of the soaring building, designed by Gustave Eiffel (yes him). The U-shaped, stainless steel bar was created by Vaughan Yates and equipped by Eric Fossard.

Americans have a long history of improvising bars. The writer Louise A. K. S. Clappe spent some time with gold prospectors in California in the 1850s and marveled at how they built bars from packing cases. You can see this pioneer spirit in television programs such as *M*A*S*H*, in which the doctors in Korea rig up a bar in a hospital tent. Or more recently in the cartoon *Family Guy*—the hero Peter Griffin builds a bar in his basement when he is under house arrest. His man cave bar evolves into a Prohibition-style nightclub when his wife begins to draw crowds with her risqué singing.

So in the words of Cole Porter, when decorating your speakeasy "Anything Goes." Old barrels can double as tables or perhaps green baize card tables, because as you're drinking illegally, you might as well be gambling. To sit on, some wooden stools and old leather sofas would look good, as would easy chairs that have seen better days. Scour junk shops for old church pews, movie theater seats or even barber's chairs. In fact, why not dress up your speakeasy as an old-time barbershop? Many speakeasies could be turned into something more innocent when warning came of a raid.

The great thing about the urban speakeasy look is it can be a bit rough around the edges. If you don't want to do it yourself, there are lots of companies now that make furniture in wood and metal from reclaimed materials. Just please no pristine stripped pine, especially on the walls; you want it to look like a bar, not a sauna.

Designer Vivien Leone's New York apartment features an elegant wood-paneled corner bar complemented by a yin and yang occasional table (*below*). A cellar you can entertain in is every wine lover's dream (*opposite, below*). This cool (in both senses of the word) basement room is in the home of German designer Marc Meiré. It is lined on three sides with wood, and the fourth is made of glass so he can admire his precious collection.

Fire in the hole! The nautical theme of The Bowery, a live music venue in Dublin, has been created by lining the walls with rough-hewn planking reclaimed from a local convent and portholes from the decommissioned Irish naval ship *Le Setanta* (**above left**). Classic pub look with a twist (**above right**). This is from Ape & Bird, a former central London pub. The bar itself looks great with its contrasting polished wood top.

A good bar doesn't have to be fancy or even designed (*right*). Quite the opposite sometimes. With its black-painted brick wall, rudimentary industrial shelving, and rather ramshackle feel, you get the sense that this place has accumulated items and character over the years. For that authentic Prohibition feel you could even offer your guests substandard booze out of teacups, though I wouldn't recommend it if you want them to return.

THE TROPICAL LOOK—TIKI BARS

One of the most popular ways to deck out your home bar is to go for the Tiki look. There's a whole subculture, with blogs, magazines, chatrooms, and suppliers devoted to it. The word comes from Polynesian mythology—Tiki was the name of the first man—but Tiki as a bar culture owes far more to California than Hawaii.

The two godfathers of Tiki were Ernest Raymond Beaumont Gantt, better known as Don the Beachcomber, who opened an eponymous bar in Hollywood in 1934, and "Trader" Vic Bergstrom, who opened a bar in Oakland in northern California that became Trader Vic's. Both offered a blend of tropical decor, strong rum-based cocktails and, for some reason, Chinese food—I suppose anything exotic would do. They both proved immensely popular and grew into chains. The Trader Vic's in the Beverly Hills Hotel opened in 1955, and became one of the city's most fashionable nightspots.

There were legions of imitators, perhaps because the look was cheap to copy. You just needed some tribal masks, lots of bamboo, grass mats, and to offer cocktails such as Zombies and Mai Tais (from a Tahitian word meaning good.) The Tiki look spread across the world in the '50s and '60s. There

No you're not in Hawaii, but beneath the streets of downtown Chicago (*right*). With a drinks list created by Kevin Beary, Three Dots and a Dash is the Windy City's premier Tiki bar. No surprise then that it was named one of the World's 50 Best Bars by *Drinks International* magazine.

can be few cities that didn't have a Tiki bar—there were even whole Tiki hotels. Probably the most famous was the Tonga Room at the Fairmont Hotel in San Francisco, with its swimming pool and beach huts. In the 1960s scenes of Martin Scorsese's *Goodfellas* (1990), Ray Liotta and Joe Pesci hang out in a fellow mobster's New York Tiki bar, which they later torch for the insurance money.

The Tiki look was as much a defining symbol of prosperous '50s America as mid-century modern. It was common for swinging suburban Americans to have a Tiki bar in their basement or garage. The Tiki boom slowed in the '70s and '80s: the last Don the Beachcomber closed in the '80s. Trader Vic's are still going, mainly in the Middle East. The

Beverly Hills venue closed in 2017, but many of the original bars, such as the one that opened in the Park Lane Hilton, London in 1963, are still thriving.

Just as with lounge bars, there was a Tiki revival in the 1990s. In fact, the two go hand in hand. They're both a celebration of "square" culture from the '40s and '50s. Tiki, though, is more about fantasy, so don't get too carried away with authenticity; Tiki is a '40s Hollywood take on island culture than the real Polynesia. That goes for music, too, essential for the Tiki feel. You could listen to Hawaiian musicians such as Don Ho or Israel Kamakawiwo'ole, but remember that exotic-sounding music from musicians with prosaic names is much more Tiki. Look out for artists like

Hello. Again.

Arthur Lyman, Martin Denny, and Les Baxter, who blended tribal rhythms with easy listening. Californian surf music, like Dick Dale or the Beach Boys, would work, too.

For that proper escapist feel, you need darkness: a Tiki bar should be cave-like with very little natural light. Though it goes without saying that Tiki works very well outdoors if the weather gods smile on you. If you are set on the Tiki look, there is no shortage of suppliers to help you. One thing it's important to note is that there's not much point having just a bar, as you might with a mid-century cocktail cabinet. With Tiki you really have to go whole hog. If you don't have a basement, garage, or swimming pool to devote to Tiki, then it's probably best not to bother. There's no room for minimalism: you need grass mats on the walls, puffer fish, tribal masks, fake palm trees, bamboo, Hawaiian shirts: the whole kit and caboodle. In the '50s and '60s an American company Witco (Western International Trading Company) imported Polynesian furniture and knick knacks

into the US, or got American designers to create furniture in a Tiki style. Some of the best stuff now goes for a lot of money on eBay.

A more restrained tropical feel can be achieved by aping the colonial look of clubs in British India and Malaysia, many of which are still going. Think lots of bamboo, ceiling fans, and sepia photos of men in pith helmets or magnificently turbanned maharajas. If, however, your heart is set on Tiki, a word of warning: it may begin to take over your life. You might find yourself on a cold winter night in a Hawaiian shirt, Mai Tai in hand, shaking your bottom to *The Exotic Moods* of Les Baxter.

The Mahiki bar in Mayfair, London has been the haunt of the international jet set since it opened in 2005, with regulars including Prince Harry and Paris Hilton (*opposite*). It's named after the Polynesian path to the underworld and majors on the classic Tiki bar array of rum-based cocktails.

This drinks tray in interior designer Hubert Zandberg's Berlin apartment holds an enviable collection of kitsch glassware (*above*).

This simple beach bar on Harbour Island in the Bahamas was designed by India Hicks (*right*). The counter and shelving are constructed from varnished planks of wood, and the rum selection is, as you might expect, extensive.

RETRO STYLE

When I mentioned to friends that I was writing a book about home bars, the most common response was, oh my parents/grandparents/swinging uncle used to have one of those globe cocktail cabinets. It is such an icon of 1970s interior design that in the '80s and '90s the globe cocktail cabinet became a shorthand on film or in advertising for bad taste, along with those wicker chairs that can be suspended from the ceiling.

For many, the '70s are an embarrassment, but before you dismiss this era remember that in the '50s and '60s, Art Deco was once considered in a similar way, and mid-century modern furniture until quite recently was worthless junk. I prefer to think of the '70s as a reaction to the stifling tastefulness of modernism. Out went all that minimalist Scandinavian stuff and in came… well, everything: pop art, Victoriana, bamboo, shag pile, avocado bathrooms, and lots and lots of orange. This change began earlier than the '70s. You can see the minimalism of the '50s begin to disappear in the films of the 1960s. Think of Michael Caine's Portobello Road gaff in *The Italian Job* (1969), which looks more like a bric-a-brac shop than a bachelor pad, or the eclecticism of the cover of the Beatles' *Sergeant Pepper's Lonely Hearts Club Band* (1967).

You can see this progression when searching for a vintage home bar. From wood veneer and Formica in the 1950s, bar designs gradually becameg more outrageous in the late '50s and '60s with bamboo, plastic or bars shaped like the prow of ships. From the early '70s one can find padded bars in burgundy velour with built-in 8-track stereos. Lurid bar accessories are very 1970s. I can remember my parents having pink elephant ice cubes and sexy lady stirrers. But these kinds of things were available much earlier; not everyone in the '50s was living in mid-century splendor. In his (not entirely serious) 1951 book *The Hour*, American historian, Bernard DeVoto rails against people who bring "whimsy and liquor and nudity together" when making drinks. Sounds like a '70s bachelor pad.

It is, however, difficult to generalize about '70s taste because it was a contradictory decade. It was a time of manmade fabrics when any kind of interpersonal contact might result in an electric shock, but it was also the era of stripped pine, crazy paving and the back-to-nature movement. This dichotomy is best expressed in the BBC sitcom *The Good Life* (1975), in which two couples live next door to each other in suburban Surrey: the corduroy-wearing Goods, who have given up the rat race to grow organic vegetables in their garden, and the aspirational polyester-clad gin and tonic swilling Leadbetters. To make things even more '70s there's a subtle swinging undercurrent, as Tom and Jerry (the names are entirely intentional), rather fancy each other's wives, Barbara and Margo. The American equivalent would be the sitcom *Green Acres*, which ran until 1971. In it a high-powered attorney escapes the rat race by becoming a farmer, dragging his reluctant wife played by Eva Gabor (sister of Zsa Zsa) away from the Manhattan life she loves.

A bar with its feet very firmly in the 1950s (**opposite**). This retro-style bar is inspired by the classic roadside diner. Everything from the chromium-plated counter, the swivelling stools fixed to the floor and checkerboard pattern screams rock 'n' roll.

So when searching for the right '70s bar, you have a multitude of looks to choose from: it could be futuristic with glass bricks, chrome and plastic, it might be made from bamboo or padded leather or vinyl. You could go for the pop art look by recycling an old television into a cocktail cabinet, or make a feature out of wood veneer record player or shag pile rug. though perhaps not in bright orange. You don't need to go for the full '70s lifestyle though. Most '70s home bars would work in a modern living room. The best thing is that you can still pick these things up cheaply, and they make such a refreshing change from the ubiquitous Ikea or the bland beige boutique hotel look.

Whatever you do remember, there's a sense of liberation about '70s design. It was a decade when people were literally letting their hair down. It was an age of self-expression and individualism, when the anything goes values of the '60s percolated down to the suburbs. Hence all that swinging.

There's a sort of 1970s Scandinavian hunting lodge feel going on with this chalet designed by Ken Fulk (*left*). With its pine-clad floor and staircase, and elegant but well-equipped little bar, it's just the kind of place where you wouldn't mind getting snowed in.

Taking its inspiration from '60s science fiction, this bar (*above*) was created by interior designer Martyn Lawrence Bullard for Tommy Hilfiger and his wife Dee in their Miami beachside property. You can't ignore those space-age acrylic Lucite bar stools, and neon art by Tracey Emin provides a contemporary touch.

A little bit of '50s American suburbia in modern Cape Town (*opposite*). Interior designer Trevor Dykman has combined an elegant Formica-topped bar with local touches—a game trophy and vintage South African travel poster—all set off beautifully by the stark white walls. And who could resist anything served from that giant silver ice bucket!

This has to be the ultimate 1970s playboy pad (*right*). That lounger in the front of the picture has a built-in cocktail bar, stereo, and television. One can imagine Roger Moore bursting into the room resplendent in a powder blue safari suit.

A pair of decidedly 1970s-looking orange plastic Magis Bombo bar stools by Stefano Giovannoni grace this curved contemporary bar against a floral signature wall in the living room of a private home (*below*).

Owner and designer Bryan Graybill devised this piece as a "cocktail sofa" to entertain friends in his Miami living room (*opposite, top*). It consists of a daybed made from ivory and pink microsuede in a curved banquette that wraps around a table. In a crook between the two sits a well-stocked circular bar.

This bar was originally a vaulted stone *bergerie*, or sheep barn (*opposite, below*). The property in the south of France was reinvented by American designer Ken Fulk and the barn furnished with a fully equipped bar.

The "Q-Series" bar in brushed and mirrored stainless steel by Quench Home Bars looks purposeful and discreet in this lavish contemporary attic lounge area designed by Penelope Allen Design (*overleaf*) .

POOLSIDE PLEASURES

Can there be a better way to spend a summer's afternoon than lazing around by the pool soaking up the sun and having a few drinks? Whether it's just you and a Robert Ludlum thriller that you've dropped in the water a couple of times, your family, or you've invited 150 people over, nothing takes the edge off the heat better than an ice-cold Heineken, a gin and tonic, or a frozen raspberry Daiquiri. In the sunshine everything tastes better, as long as it is cold, wet, and alcoholic.

At the most basic level your poolside "home bar" could just consist of a cooler filled with ice, beer, champagne, and maybe even a soft drink or two. You don't want to overdo it in the heat. From there the next stage would be a poolside bar cart. This can be not dissimilar to an indoor one, but it must have a large icebox and needs to be robust enough to take whatever the elements or small children can throw at it, so no easily marked wood veneers or flimsy glass shelves. You can buy some simple models in rattan or elaborate custom-built wooden versions with built-in racks for glasses and cocktail tools.

If you're lucky enough to live in Florida or similarly sunny climes, you'll be using your poolside bar all year round, but for most of us it will be a summer thing only, so you need something that can be put away/covered up/shut up for the winter, which is why a wooden cart or simple credenza is ideal. Or if you're feeling particularly outrageous how about a glow-in-the-dark portable bar made from luminous plastic by Italian industrial designer Giò Colonna Romano? Perfect for those Hollywood pool parties.

Even better though, would be to have a built-in catering area with a barbecue, outdoor kitchen, and fully stocked bar—and don't forget that a refrigerator with a freezer compartment is essential for poolside refreshment. You could get something built in red terracotta decorated with Mexican ceramic tiles. Or take it even further and put in a fountain, cacti, and flowering plants for that Hacienda look. Or perhaps a Jamaican rum shack, with sun-faded wood and colorful hand-painted advertisements for Wray & Nephew overproof rum and Red Stripe beer. Then when you shut up shop in winter hang up a sign saying "gone fishing."

The only problem with a bar like this is that it requires getting out of the pool to refresh your drink, so how about a swim-up bar, complete with bar stools in the water? Here a tropical theme would look splendid, with a thatched roof. In fact why not take it further with a whole Tiki-themed swimming pool area complete with bar, sound system, hula dancers, beach huts, and parrots flying around? See pages 54–9 for inspiration.

A minimal concrete bar area has been created in this outdoor space in a French country house, with archways opening onto a formal garden (*opposite, top left*).

You can't really have a tropical bar without a palm tree. This one sits in the center of the outdoor bar, offering shade to thirsty drinkers and the bartender alike (*opposite, top right*).

Thanks to the sliding glass doors this indoor bar in a luxury apartment can, at the touch of a button, become an outdoor bar, so guests enjoying the infinity pool can refresh their drinks (*opposite, below*).

Or what about those swanky Balearic hotels where well-heeled ravers in white linen trousers drink magnums of Whispering Angel Provençal Rosé and dance to laid-back beats. For that Café del Mar look you'll need enormous comfy all-outdoor sofas, with blankets for when it gets chilly and tented cover. When the sun goes down, candles and soft lighting provide a sympathetic glow for ravers who remember when house music was young.

But for the ultimate in poolside glamour go a little further back in time to the 1930s yacht set. Take your inspiration from the lines of those gorgeous pre-war speedboats made by Riva or Chris Craft, with their polished wood and brass. You'll recognize them from the Venice boat chase in *Indiana Jones and the Last Crusade* (1989). If you've got the space you could even go as far as the Pacific Seas bar at Clifton's Republic Hotel in downtown

Los Angeles, which has an entire wooden speedboat in the room. And for those on more limited means who still want the nautical look, you can buy '60s and '70s cocktail cabinets or bars that look like the prow of a boat. Then put on white trousers, a blazer and your Cap'n hat and pretend you're Tony Curtis pretending to be a millionaire in *Some Like it Hot* (1959). You don't even need a swimming pool.

A drinks tray in the garden of British designer John Stefanidis's house on the Greek island of Patmos (**above**). It is now one of the fashionable islands in the Aegean, but John has had a house here since the 1960s.

With its sun-bleached wood and dried palm fronds draped across the roof, this outdoor tropical bar has a rustic, relaxed feel (**opposite**). Perfect for beach or poolside drinking. I bet they do a mean rum punch.

A well-equipped poolside bar has been built into the overall structure of this whitewashed summer villa on the island of Ibiza, overlooking the Mediterranean (*above*). You can almost smell the rosemary.

You can really live the modernist dream at this house in Marfa, Texas by architect Allen Bianchi (*overleaf*) . The courtyard swimming pool is furnished with an outdoor bar and dining area designed by Barbara Hill.

A stylish outdoor dining area complete with Philippe Starck armchairs
(*above*). It features not only a recessed bar area with a stone sink, but also
an Italian bar cart, so you're never more than an arm's reach away from a
perfectly made drink.

THE PROFESSIONAL LOOK

Home bars are essentially about showing off. Nothing wrong with that. It's about making a feature of your drinks, demonstrating your cocktail prowess and turning friends popping over for a drink into an event. But what if you're more interested in the drinks themselves? What if your bar is above all a place for you to hone your skills? Well then, perhaps you want something that looks more like a professional bar.

You'll need everything in the right place: compartments for ice, a big freezer to keep bottles and glasses cold, and plenty of counter surface for chopping. I've always loved the no-nonsense look of the classic Spanish tapas bar. These are often very basic affairs, with a marble bar top and then white or patterned tiles behind. Everything is there for a reason and can be easily cleaned. Something this practical, even a little clinical, would look great in a modern house or a villa.

The next step would be to create your very own cocktail laboratory. In the late 2000s, cocktail making became a lot more complicated. Inspired by the molecular gastronomy movement made

The American Bar at the Savoy Hotel in London has been serving excellent cocktails since 1904 (*left*). It closed for refurbishment in 2007, reopened in 2010, and in 2017 was officially recognised as the best bar in the world at The World's 50 Best Bars awards.

famous by Ferran Adrià's restaurant elBulli in Spain or Heston Blumenthal's Fat Duck in Bray, Berkshire, bartenders such as Tony Conigliaro at 69 Colebrooke Row in London began working more like scientists or perhaps alchemists than traditional bartenders.

Tony has a special laboratory up the road from the bar that is like a boozy Willy Wonka's chocolate factory. There he makes his own ingredients, infusions, bitters, and so on, and some he ages for a mature flavor, like whisky. I remember trying something called a "Woodland Martini" made with sherry, gin, and a special bitters made from leaves and things found on the forest floor, which totally transformed my view of what a cocktail could be. It was like walking through a wood in the Fall. This new breed of bartenders were described as "mixologists," a word that was originally coined in 19th-century America to describe the early cocktail pioneers. It's not a word I use much, but it does point to a truth: people like Tony were doing a whole lot more than just making drinks behind a bar.

So the bar has been raised, if you'll excuse the pun, but where does that leave the home bartender? Even if you're deadly serious about cocktails you are unlikely to want to invest in dehydrators, sous-vide equipment, centrifuges, distillation apparatus, and an ice cream machine (though we will look at such things in the next chapter). But there's no reason why you shouldn't try to recreate the clinical look in your house.

There's a company in the UK called Quench who design home bars in stainless steel with built-in sinks, refrigerators, and freezers, which would not look out of place in a professional set-up (see pages 100 and 110). This look is now very popular in domestic kitchens: think lots of stainless steel, big industrial-style burners, and chunky high-pressure taps. You can buy stainless-steel work counters from junk shops and secondhand professional kitchen equipment suppliers. So the thought occurs to me that if you're serious about cocktails, you probably have a well-equipped kitchen with almost everything you need in place.

Come to think of it you might already have a bar at home without realizing it. Many modern interiors have an open plan kitchen and living room. In my last apartment the living room was knocked through to the kitchen with just a kitchen counter separating them. Voila! A home bar! This way you don't have to double up on knives, etc. To finish, get a shelf fitted above head level for bottles and glasses, and you're starting to look pretty professional. Now you can hone your bartending skills and impress your friends at the same time. You could even wear a lab coat, but don't describe yourself as a mixologist, or people will laugh at you behind your back.

This elegant bar at Nios restaurant in the Muse Hotel near Times Square in New York is a contemporary design but shows a strong Art Deco influence (**opposite**). The giant wine refrigerator adds a dramatic touch.

Another bar that makes a feature of wine storage (*above*). This is the work of American designer Nicole Hollis. The eye-catching glass-fronted wine cabinet provides a backdrop to a marble-topped kitchen island that doubles as a bar.

This is a beautiful use of a small space from German designer Marc Meiré (*opposite*). The minimal kitchen is set off by matte black wood-clad walls and a zinc counter on white kitchen units. Note the enormous bin under the counter, probably for all those empties.

This modern kitchen/bar area is furnished with contemporary bar stools and overlooks a spectacular city skyline (*above left*). Cantilevered stainless steel shelves slotted between a pair of kitchen cabinets house glassware and bottles (*above right*). A free-standing bar opens onto a swimming pool terrace with a view of the ocean (*below*). This California home has an open plan, sunken bar area, topped with a marble counter edged in natural leather (*opposite*).

DRINKS CUPBOARDS
AND COCKTAIL CABINETS

Perhaps cinema's greatest office is in *Sabrina* (1954), starring Audrey Hepburn as Sabrina Fairchild and Humphrey Bogart as Linus Larrabee. It consists of an enormous boardroom with a window overlooking the Hudson River, and a very cool elaborate-looking PA system all decked out in sleek mid-century wood. But the thing that really caught my eye was what can only be described as a cocktail kitchenette, with cupboard, a sink, and a cocktail shaker in the corner of the office, from where Bogart whips them both up a frozen Daiquiri.

This is the cocktail cabinet dream: elegant discretion. It should be to all intents and purposes a hidden bar. A corner bar in your living room or a cart are about showing off, whereas a cocktail cabinet just sits there quietly until it is needed. You

might not even know its purpose until the clock comes 'round to 6 o'clock (or let's face it 5 o'clock) and it's time for a cocktail.

This discretion is not accidental: a cocktail cabinet has its origins in a sturdy piece of furniture in which you could lock your precious booze away from prying hands. In Victorian times the well off had cabinets with a special compartment for an enormous block of ice so that they could offer chilled champagne or Sherry Cobblers to guests. Such furniture really came into its own during Prohibition. One could buy cocktail cabinets disguised as a radio, a desk, or even a piano. Or trunks and suitcases that at the flick of a switch turned into cocktail bars. In the '20s and '30s, as the cocktail boom took off across the world, you could buy Art Deco cabinets that opened up into alcoholic wonderlands, with mirrored surfaces, internal lighting, glasses, and decanters. It's unusual to find these now with fixtures and fittings intact.

You wouldn't ever need to leave the house with one of these beauties (*left*). It's a Tele-Bar made by Admiral in the 1950s and combines a television, radio, record player, and, of course, a fully stocked bar. The lid turns into a serving tray for cocktails. They are now much-sought-after collector's items.

A drinks cabinet created especially for this living room by San Francisco-based designer Nicole Hollis (*opposite*). There's space for every kind of bottle and the doors hold an array of glasses. The highly polished doors reflect the room, and it's lockable to keep out prying children.

There's a great mixture of new and old in this dining room designed by Ken Fulk (*overleaf*). The drinks cabinet is an original mid-century number with a foldout tray. The rest of the furniture is more modern.

Art Deco cocktail cabinets were for the wealthy, but after World War II, cocktail cabinets became almost de rigueur in modern homes. The look changed to what we would now call mid-century: Scandinavian or Scandinavian-inspired designs with clean lines, and bare wood mixed with glass, metal, and modern plastics such as Formica. Look out for names such as Felix Augenfeld in the US or, in Britain, A.M. Lewis, who designed furniture for Liberty. These might be plain or highly decorative, with lacquered wood designs. Some might be entire home entertainment systems, combining a bar with a built-in turntable, radio, and even reel-to-reel tape player. Prices for the top mid-century designs, especially the original Danish stuff, have increased dramatically in recent years, but you can still find bargains. Many were mass-produced for an increasingly wealthy suburban middle class, not just in Europe and the US but South America, Japan and all over the world.

If you can't source the mid-century cocktail cabinet of your dreams or find that it's out of your price range, don't worry. You can pretend that almost any sideboard or cupboard is in fact a cocktail cabinet. It just needs to be tall enough to hold bottles and you have a home bar.

Though not designed specifically as a cocktail cabinet, this distressed black lacquer wooden cabinet with a burgundy interior does the job perfectly (*above left*). It shows off a collection of bottles, decanters, and glasses in a corner of this English country kitchen.

Painted a soft blue and with generous metal shelving fitted against a deep window, this former cupboard has been transformed into an elegant drinks cabinet in the London home of designer Hubert Zandberg (*above*).

Another lesson in how anything can be a bar (*opposite*). In designer Nicky Haslam's London sitting room, one of a pair of "Swedish stoves" conceals rusty Victorian pipes and its twin, seen here, is a bar and china cupboard.

A traditional drinks display in the library of designer Nicky Haslam's home in the heart of the English countryside (*opposite*). The portrait of his mother is by Scottish artist Robin Guthrie

What do you mean you don't have room for all those bottles? This kitchen bottle rack shows you how it can be done, no matter how small your pad is (*left*).

Wicker was big in the 1970s. Here a matching retro bar and chair are given a light modern twist with a white painted wall and shutter (*below left*). And that alcove has found its perfect function as a place to display bottles.

How to disguise your bar as a sauna. That pine cladding opens to reveal a concealed bar area with shelves of glasses and a small sink behind a curved metal bar and vintage bar stools (*below*).

This retro drinks cabinet is designed to open to create a mono-pod serving table and reveal glass shelving for glassware and bottles (*above*).

A great bit of industrial design here (*opposite*). This cabinet was salvaged from a French factory. It has been refurbished into a chic cocktail cabinet that shows off your bottles and equipment to good effect.

An antique drinks cabinet with lacquered wood and a hinged glass shelf (*above*). There's lots of storage space for glasses and bottles and it can all be tidied away when you're feeling abstemious.

Often the best bars are the hidden ones. This clandestine drinks cabinet concealed behind double doors clad in *verre églomisé* was designed by legendary British designer, writer, and socialite Nicky Haslam (*opposite*).

TROLLEYS, BAR CARTS, AND TRAYS

It's always a shame when you are visiting someone you haven't seen for ages and they spend the entire time in the kitchen cooking. Just so with drinks. The joy of the home bar is that while preparing elaborate, or not so elaborate, cocktails you can still chat with your guests. Even if you don't have space for a proper home bar never fear, because you can bring the bar to your guests.

At the most basic level there is the drinks tray. This should be large enough to hold three or four bottles, glasses, and, most importantly, a bucket for ice and a bottle cooler. Then you can wow your guests with your cocktail-making prowess. As there isn't much space, it's probably best to limit the choices to drinks based on the same spirit. So, for example, you could offer Martinis, Negronis, and Americanos with only four bottles, a soda syphon, an orange, and a lemon.

A drinks tray is a good way of displaying bottles to show what you have on offer, but in the office it also makes a statement. If you look in the background in offices in old films there will almost always be a drinks tray. The suggestion is that we work hard here, but we play hard too. Trays should be big and sturdy, ideally with handles, while a round silver-plated tray with a lip gives that classic Jeeves look. But you don't need a purpose-made tray: one of those enormous old Ricard ashtrays would work well, or a wooden wine box with its high sides is also perfect.

If you want a bit of theater, though, you really need a bar cart, or what the British would call a drinks trolley. Davanti Enoteca in Chicago has a lavishly stocked Bloody Mary trolley, at Bourbon Steak in New York they have a gold-rimmed bar cart offering bourbon (naturally) and Japanese whiskies, and at the Oxo Tower in London they have a Martini trolley so big and lavish that it could double as a yacht. But at one of London's smartest addresses, Dukes London in St James's, the head bartender, Alessandro Palazzi, has something a little more understated. Dukes is a converted private home, so it doesn't have the huge spaces of the Savoy or the Dorchester. Therefore the trolley has to be small. Alessandro designed it himself; it's an unassuming wooden thing with three layers and small robust castors which makes it highly maneuverable.

If you're in the market for a trolley you should ask yourself if you need it to store all your liquor or if you are just going to use it to entertain. How big is your home and how much will you actually be wheeling it about? Castors are preferable to wheels. Some have lift-off shelves that are all very well, but make sure they are sturdy. Nobody likes a wobbly trolley. If you go to secondhand stores in less salubrious parts of town you should be able to pick up a good bar cart for not much money. Many homes had them in the '60s and '70s, but then they went out of fashion. Old catering or hospital trolleys can provide a bit of utilitarian chic and they are built to last. If money's no object then the Finnish Alvar Aalto model in stripped

I have a feeling that the owner of this vintage cart has a sense of fun and a love of rum-based cocktails (*opposite*). There are Tiki mugs, kitsch memorabilia, and even a pineapple ice bucket.

wood and laminate is gorgeous, or if you're looking for something a bit more Deco then the polished nickel Connaught bar cart by DwellStudio (named after the hotel naturally) is quite magnificent. If you want the Scandi look for not too many kroner then the Milo bar cart, named after mid-century designer Milo Baughman has castors so it is very manoeuvrable and makes a great piece of furniture. Finally, Ikea does a Råskog cart in utilitarian metal that has three layers with deep trays to keep your booze and glasses safe. It offers unbeatable value—as long as you're good at putting things together.

It's very hard for guests to say no when the trolley is in front of them and it's ideal for the picky, as they can specify their drink just how they want it. According to Alessandro Palazzi, he introduced the trolley to Dukes in order to reassure American customers who worried about the quality of the British Martini: "They see the frozen gin bottle and you can see them relax into their chairs."

"The Gin Trolley" by Quench Home Bars is the ultimate accessory for the modern gin lover (*above right*). Made from high-gloss laminated birch ply and polished acrylic, it contains a refrigerator, a countertop, and of course space for many, many gin bottles.

This fine example of a mid-century bar cart in designer Hubert Zandberg's Berlin apartment was designed by Brazilian Sergio Rodrigues (*right*). Note the castors for maximum maneuverability.

A lesson in how to turn serving drinks into an art form with beautiful engraved Martini glasses, a silver tray with a napkin, and an array of delicious salty snacks. All you need it a butler to serve you (*opposite, top*).

Against an artwork by Gert & Uwe Tobias, a monochrome mood is set by a drinks tray with a black glass decanter on the black countertop of this French kitchen by designer Hubert Zandberg (*opposite, below*).

In the foreground of the living room in an apartment decorated by Ken Fulk there's a real showstopper of a bar cart with large carriage wheels (**opposite**). Even with an enormous bouquet of flowers there's room here for a serious bottle collection. Behind is a glass-fronted cabinet filled with books and collectables.

You could hardly refuse a drink when confronted with such magnificence (**below**). In this dining room of a London apartment the spirits are presented in cut crystal decanters on a gilded "crane table" by Meret Oppenheim. The sliding door behind is made of copper and the floor is Connolly leather.

An antique billiard table in this rustic living room provides a convenient surface for serving drinks (*above*). That is, until somebody feels inclined to a game.

A shabby chic wooden table in the bright airy pavilion of designer Nicky Haslam's country home displays a well-stocked drinks tray (*above*).

A collection of framed black and white photographs are propped up behind a generously stocked drinks tray on a granite-topped chest of drawers in a corner of designer David Jimenez's San Francisco apartment (*opposite*).

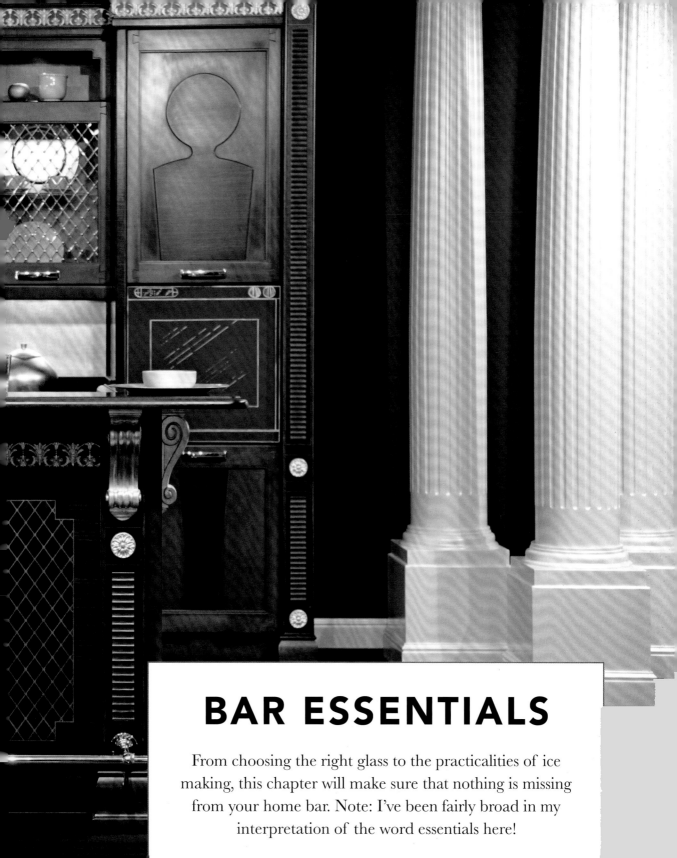

BAR ESSENTIALS

From choosing the right glass to the practicalities of ice making, this chapter will make sure that nothing is missing from your home bar. Note: I've been fairly broad in my interpretation of the word essentials here!

There are things here that you literally cannot do without, such as a cocktail shaker or a kitchen knife, but there are also things, such as a still or wooden barrels, that will take your home bar to a professional level.

1

BRINGING IT ALL BACK HOME

Designing your bar

2

KEEPING IT COOL

Refrigerators, freezers, and ice

3

SETTING UP

Bar equipment basics

4

TOP GEAR

Professional-level equipment

A pair of thoroughly industrial looking metal vintage bar stools look particularly stylish against the stark lines of the black metal bar (**opposite**).

This bar is furnished in traditional style with lots of dark wood and silver gilt, but look carefully and you'll see that behind it is thoroughly up-to-date with everything you need to make the classic cocktails (**previous pages**).

BRINGING IT ALL BACK HOME
designing your bar

The first question when designing your dream bar has to be, where am I going to put the damn thing? For the lucky few this will be a dedicated bar room, but for most of us this will more likely mean the living room, though you could put it in your bedroom for when you can't sleep. You could even, as an American boxer has done, put one in your bathroom in case you fancy a Negroni while performing your ablutions (and who doesn't get this urge sometimes?) Don't, though, do as the father of a friend of mine did, which was to put an enormous wooden pub-style bar in his small suburban living room. A bar should complement your room, not dominate it.

So your home bar needs to be the right size, and also the right height, so that you don't throw your back out slicing limes. Next, you need to think about practical matters when siting it, such as is there a plentiful source of electricity? You'll need enough socket space to plug in a refrigerator, a freezer, and lighting, not to mention blenders, and more esoteric equipment such as sous-vide baths and rotary evaporators. And don't forget about plumbing—a proper bar should have a sink. Then what kind of surface do you want on the bar? I've always hankered after those zinc-topped bars that you get in French cafés. This section will talk you through the practicalities of creating your dream home bar, covering everything from glass selection and storage to displaying your bottles to maximum effect. Just remember that a home bar doesn't have to be complicated—it should be about entertaining your guests not boring them.

What goes with the bar is equally important, such as comfortable chairs, bar stools, and banquettes. Use lamps to create the right mood; everyone looks beautiful in soft lighting, especially after a couple of drinks. But man (and woman) cannot live by alcohol alone—we need other forms of fun. You could turn your bar room into a play space, with a home movie theater, music system, pinball, video games, or, for those who prefer more sedate forms of entertainment, a bar billiard table and a library so you can lose yourself in a good book while having a drink. You could even go whole hog and transform the room into a nightclub, like top socialite Paris Hilton has in her home, though perhaps not if you live in a suburban duplex.

A bespoke 6-foot (1.8m) corner bar with gloss black acrylic front panels, designed by Quench Home Bars (*opposite*). The shelves behind light up to display the bottles to maximum effect and the lighting can be changed by remote control.

Bar surfaces

Probably your first question when putting a bar in your home is what sort of surface do I want on the bartop? It needs to be smooth and easy to wipe down. Do you want it to remain shiny and new, or to take on the patina of age? Materials such as stainless steel or the classic bar surface, zinc, don't need polishing. In fact they start to look better with age. Other materials that don't need work include marble or, for that '50s diner look, Formica.

Something like copper, however, which can look spectacular, needs constant work to battle against the tarnish—though again a little patina looks good. Darker woods, especially polished mahogany, look superb but they do need looking after, by polishing with oils and wood treatments. Stripped pine can look a bit sauna-esque and it will stain— and watch out for splinters.

The standard height of a bar is around 3 feet 7 inches (114cm). Anything taller or shorter won't feel right. There should be plenty of space behind it for you to crouch down and move around.

The amazingly intricate carved wooden bar at Gilgamesh in Camden, London (**opposite**). This lively pan-Asian restaurant is inspired by the ancient Sumerian poem *The Epic of Gilgamesh*.

Alexandre Ricard's home bar is a booze wonderland. Note the star anise detailing on the bar, a reference to the ingredients of Ricard pastis (*above left*). Architects and interior designers Jones Lambell have created an antique bar in this London home, with windows concealed by cedar louvered shutters (*above right*). Backlit wall cabinets display bottles, glassware, and assorted tools in this contemporary minimal bar (*below*). Rustic white-washed surfaces provide a contrast to the architectural-looking bar stools (*opposite*). It feels like a cave inhabited by design-savvy Scandinavians.

Reminiscent of Humphrey Bogart's office in *Sabrina* (1954), the Audrey Hepburn film, this gorgeous concealed folding bar extends from the wood paneling in this mid-century living room (***opposite***). There's even a built-in stereo turntable for playing some seductive jazz music.

A contemporary, metal semi-circular bar with matching bar stools is illuminated with a bank of recessed ceiling lights (***above***). Though it's up-to-date, those curves give it an Art Deco ocean liner feel.

Lighting

A small lamp on your bar is a good way to make it look more inviting, but also more professional—go to an old-school cocktail bar and I guarantee that they will have a lamp on the bar. It's worth spending money on, for example, an Art Deco style number, as it will add a bit of class. You can buy rechargeable lamps so that you don't have the cable. These are also useful for your tables if you're going for that '50s nightclub look. Downlighting built into the front of the bar looks very glamorous, especially if you coordinate it with the back bar. Lighting can show off your bottles, but make sure they don't get too hot. You don't want to cook your expensive whisky. Some specialist LED lighting systems will allow you to adjust the color and brightness by remote control.

This bar really makes a feature out of the lighting, most noticeably with the enormous glass bottle converted into a lamp (*below*). Behind the marble-topped industrial counter there is vintage shelving and, in front, comfortable, upholstered bar benches.

Exposed lightbulbs provide an industrial but also warm feel for a bar. Here they are fitted into a contemporary copper piping chandelier that doubles as a rack for wine glasses (*opposite, above*).

Softly illuminated back bar shelving highlights the selection of drink bottles and gives a sophisticated finish to this stainless steel living room bar designed by Quench Home Bars (*opposite, below*).

Behind the bar

The first thing that you notice when you walk into a bar is not the bar itself, it's the back bar—the display of bottles and glasses—so it's important to get this just right. This might be a built-in wooden structure with shelves, mirrors and drawers, or just a wall with shelves to hold the bottles. However you do it, it should be a booze wonderland, so that your guests gasp at the sheer variety. I have spent hours, weeks probably, staring in awe at bottles while nursing a drink. To really show off your bottles, you can display them on glass or acrylic shelving with adjustable lighting. Downlighting onto your bottles from the back bar will give your room that proper bar room feel.

Behind the bar you should have a preparation area at around kitchen counter height for chopping limes, etc. and drawer space for tools and kit, either below the bar or behind it. You should have a shelf at waist level with your most popular bottles—gin, bourbon, vermouth, etc.—at hand. You don't want to have to keep turning around. Glasses should be at hand level, too. Or, if your room has the height and the ceiling strength, a head-level shelf running the length of the bar would look really professional. There should also be racks for bottles underneath, but unless your bar is very big you'll probably need a closet for excess bottles and stuff. And, if you're serious about wine, a wine refrigerator or at the very least somewhere cool and dark to store your wine. Unless you have your own cellar, of course.

Neons signs have been a fixture of the urban landscape since the 1920s. Nothing says sleazy glamour quite like flickering neon. This one graces the Floridita Cuban Bar in Wardour Street in the heart of London's Soho (*right*).

There's no reason why your kitchen shouldn't double as a bar, as this photo shows (*above*). Bottles are discreetly tucked away on open shelving behind this free-standing kitchen island, ready for an impromptu cocktail party.

Either side of a refrigerated cabinet with a mirrored door especially for champagne, just some of Alexandre Ricard's priceless collection of rare and vintage bottles are displayed (*right*). On the lower shelves are vintage Ricard glasses and water jugs.

Sinks

If you have a proper bar, as opposed to a cabinet or cart, then you should make space for a sink so you can rinse knives, chopping boards, etc. as you go. Ideally this would be properly plumbed in with a faucet and water outlet, but even one that just feeds into a bucket is useful. Just don't forget to empty it at the end of the night.

Designed by Ken Fulk, this is a perfectly situated butler's pantry to prepare drinks to take into the dining room (*below*). There's a beautifully polished copper sink and on the walls hang trays for carrying cocktails to guests.

A cocktail bar and entertainment room designed by Hubert Zandberg features open glass shelving above a marble sink that can be hidden behind doors (*opposite*). Pride of place goes to an array of pineapple ice buckets.

With something of the feel of a movie mogul's bathroom, this dramatic black and white marble countertop and backsplash set the scene for this sink designed by Ken Fulk (*opposite*).

A bespoke drinks cabinet designed by interior architects Candy & Candy for this London apartment (*right*). There's room to keep all the spirits and wine you need, a refrigerator, drawers, and a sink. Best of all it can be shut away until it is needed.

Bar stools and seating

Any furniture has to work with the whole room—you could have heavy classic saloon-style bar stools or more elegant ones in chrome. For the comfort of your guests, it's nice to have ones with backs and padded seating. The velvet-covered ones from Danish company GUBI are gorgeous, with a price tag to match. For the more down-to-earth, old coffee sacks make a great covering material, especially if you're going for that beach/boho poolside look. Watch out for the bearings on swivel stools, as these can go quickly, even on some quite expensive models. Fixed seats will last longer. No-nonsense lightweight steel industrial-styles ones, such as those from Xavier Pauchard, look great and they can be moved easily. If you do have bar stools you will need a foot rail, otherwise legs will be left dangling, which nobody finds comfortable.

For your guests to sit at, I love small tables with lamps on them for that nightclub look, and built-in banquette seating, especially in the corner. But your room might not be a bar full time, so think about how easily you can convert it into a dining room or home movie theater. You might want something like a padded bench that can be easily moved.

Known for his exuberant style and layered interiors, designer Ken Fulk has created a Hollywood-style home bar with rich red leather banquettes and dark blue velvet curtains (*right*). A feature has been made out of the cabinet, which keeps wine at the perfect temperature.

Rosewood paneling and comfy leather seats give the room a cool modernist look in this home-entertainment/bar area (*above left*). Custom-made concrete worktops are furnished with vintage metal and laminate bar stools (*above right*). A display cabinet and bar made of onyx and glass is accessorized with contemporary stools (*below left*). The generous table means a drinks party can easily to turn into dinner—as long as you can clear some space (*below right*).

Unusual squat bar stools look like ultra-modern pieces for the world's biggest game of chess (*above*). Retro-style wood and metal bar stools (*below*). Understated aluminum bar stools surround this retro-style bar (*right*).

Home entertainment

How cool would it be to incorporate a home-entertainment system into your bar? I saw an amazing mid-century modern bar with a built-in state-of-the-art (circa 1968) hi fi from Bang & Olufsen. Or, more up-to-date, California-based Dream Arcades will sell you a $5,000 Kegerator Pro 60, a refrigerator and a keg with three taps plus an arcade game machine with 140 games via a 60-inch HDTV screen. None more man cave!

Beware however: technology moves pretty fast. A state-of-the-art stereo system from even 15 years ago would have a CD player and would not be easy to connect to your phone/computer/tablet to access your playlists. Twenty years ago it might have had a minidisc player. In the '70s an 8 track—a forerunner of the cassette—was the thing to have. Your bar should last a lifetime, so do you want an integrated music system that will date? Especially as you can now buy very high quality

portable music systems from the likes of Bose, and speakers are getting smaller and better the whole time. Ditto with home movie theater and gaming equipment. You probably don't want something built in. Increasingly people are converting their dining rooms into adult play (not that kind of play!) rooms with a movie theater, high-end music system, and, of course, a bar. That bar will probably be the only thing still working in 40 years time.

A very contemporary take on a classic games room. Rather than the dark wood and green baize, this room is decorated in muted shades of gray and white for a less oppressive feel (*above*).

While having a drink what could be better than a quiet game of chess? This is the green-paneled bar area of the Harrison apartments in San Francisco, designed by Ken Fulk (*opposite*).

The perfect home movie theater set up (*right*). With these incredibly comfortable-looking leather chairs with matching footstools and a Milo bar cart lurking in the background, it doesn't particularly matter what movie you see.

KEEPING IT COOL

Perhaps the most important thing when planning your home bar is to think about how you are going to keep your drinks cold. Every bar in the world should have a big sign saying: "Not enough ice or small watery cubes ruin drinks."

Cocktails depend on lots and lots of ice, much more than you'd think. Cocktails were possible in the days before artificial refrigeration because huge blocks of ice were harvested from the Great Lakes in winter (just like in the film *Frozen*) and kept insulated for the summer. Ice is the key ingredient in a cocktail, but one that is often overlooked. If you want to impress a bartender talk to him about ice. Watch a pro at work and he will not only fill the shaker with ice but the glass, too, so while he shakes, the glass chills.

For ice cutting, a Japanese knife is the tool of choice (*below left*). Japan has maintained the tradition of cutting ice blocks on the bar, and produces the best blades for the job. To create crystal-clear ice, use a machine that freezes very slowly and involves a slight motion.

A giant piece of ice will chill your drink with minimal dilution (*below left*). Perfect for appreciating the delicate flavors of a glass of Lillet Blanc. And, of course, it can't be denied that an enormous hand-carved piece of ice looks rather splendid, though it does chill the nose when you drink it.

Fountains such as these were fashionable in 19th-century Paris to dispense absinthe (*opposite*). What could be better, Pernod on tap? Not only do they deliver a glass of perfectly chilled pastis, but they look utterly splendid.

The reason you need lots of ice is that you want to make your drink cold quickly and then keep it that way without diluting it too much. If you do as most British pubs do and put one ice cube in a G&T then it will melt very quickly, ruining your drink and not making it very cold either. You should be filling the glass with ice and using cold gin, cold tonic, and, indeed, a cold glass. This way your drink will stay colder for longer, without the ice melting. Ideally you would just use one enormous ice cube as it has less surface area than lots of smaller ones, so melts slower. We'll come on to that shortly. But some rules are made to be broken: when I drink blended Scotch I sometimes add just a small ice cube because I do want dilution and I don't want my whisky too cold. Whatever floats your boat.

Beware when buying ready-made ice cubes: they usually have holes that make them melt quicker and break when shaken hard—both things that will dilute your drink. You can buy countertop ice makers from companies such as Polar that claim to make ice in about seven minutes, but it will be in that super quick-melting thimble shape.

Most modern refrigerators now have ice cube makers, which are fine for chilling water, but have some drawbacks for the home bartender. The ice will be made from tap water and the cubes themselves are usually long and thin, which means they melt more easily than an honest-to-goodness square cube. They're really fine for most people, but if you're serious about cocktails then you should be making your own ice.

So you'll need lots of ice trays, ideally rubber or silicon ones that make as large a cube as possible. Now this is going to sound prissy, but it is well worth using filtered or even bottled water for your ice. If you live in a hard water area the calcium will leave a deposit in your glass from the ice and I find the freezing process seems to accentuate any chlorine taste in the water, which is why I'm not that keen on built-in ice cube makers. If you're feeling really fancy, boiling the water before freezing removes the oxygen, which means that you get totally translucent cubes. Also hot water freezes faster than cold water—this is a principle known as the Mpemba effect, after the Tanzanian student

If your bar is on the more professional side it might have a built-in ice bucket or even a chilled tray so that your ice is always at the right temperature, as Alexandre Ricard does (**left**). Don't be tempted to try to imitate some professionals who scoop the ice up with the glass—this can chip the glass, ruining your best lead crystal tumblers and perhaps your guests' lips. Use a scoop.

All the kit you need for the perfect Dry Martini, from the Gin Trolley designed by Quench Home Bars (**opposite**). This particular Martini is being made with Sacred Gin, which is handmade in Highgate, London. Note that the vermouth is in a handy dispenser so that you can add just a drop, and the tongs to serve up the ice.

who discovered it in 1963, though it had been noted by some of history's big thinkers, including Francis Bacon, Descartes, and Aristotle.

You should budget roughly half a tray of ice for each drink, so if you're a regular cocktailer, you have to get into the habit of decanting your ice into freezer bags and making more. Or you could take a leaf out of the professional's book. You remember Sharon Stone's weapon of choice in *Basic Instinct*, the ice pick? Most British viewers will have been baffled as to why anyone would have an ice pick in the house. But for Americans it would seem obvious: to hack off bits of ice with, of course. So the professional approach is to freeze big blocks of ice—you can use Tupperware or baking trays as containers—and then (carefully) channel your inner Sharon Stone with an ice pick or just something strong and sharp. It's best to do this while sober. Some more outré bartenders use a chainsaw to sculpt enormous cubes in interesting shapes. Probably best not to try this at home.

The latest trend in ice is to have one enormous perfectly spherical lump so that you have the minimum surface area of ice-to-drink ratio, which means slow melting. And indeed it does work, though I find that the enormous sphere bangs against my nose and makes it harder to actually drink the drink. It seems to me to be taking ice nerdiness a step too far. Nevertheless if you want to get the pro look you can buy molds in which to make spherical ice cubes which range from inexpensive plastic affairs to machined aluminum Japanese numbers for around $100 (from Williams Sonoma) that pressure a piece of ice into a completely translucent perfect sphere.

Then you'll need somewhere to keep your ice cold, which for most of us will mean an ice bucket. I

remember these dispiriting things in traditional English pubs, which would contain a cold liquid with small pieces of ice floating in it. Don't treat your ice bucket like this. Keep the lid on, if it has one, and refresh it often. It could be an open metal bucket like you would use for champagne or an insulated plastic or metal affair with a snug-fitting lid, which will keep your ice frozen for longer. Some have an inner lining with holes in so that the ice doesn't sit in meltwater. You can buy fabulous kitsch ones in the shape of pineapples, Art Deco metal ones that look like rocket ships, and branded champagne buckets. I'm particularly fond of Bakelite Thermos ice buckets from the 1950s. You might want to go the full Jeeves and use tongs to remove the cubes with style.

Useful in a similar vein are those vacuum or earthenware coolers for wine bottles or jackets that you keep in the freezer and then put around a bottle for quick chilling.

Kingsley Amis would certainly approve: an entire refrigerator devoted to drink (*above*). Next to it
are built-in brick shelves to store your wine, while the entire room is kept cool behind glass doors.

Refrigerators and freezers

Kingsley Amis thought for the serious booze enthusiast a refrigerator devoted to drink was essential. He wrote: "wives and such are constantly filling up any refrigerator they have a claim on, even its ice-compartment, with irrelevant rubbish like food." If you have space for one electric item under your bar, make it a refrigerator, ideally with an ice compartment. You can buy very small ones to store a few bottles of wine, champagne, your gin, some mixers, and a couple trays of ice. If you're into beer then you'll need a refrigerator devoted to the stuff. This could be in a separate room, but a double-doored Cornelius Zenith display refrigerator would show off your range of unusual Belgian beers with some style.

If your home bar is outside you are going to need a more robust piece of equipment that can stand up to the elements and with a powerful motor to deal with all that heat. A tiny countertop refrigerator will struggle in a Californian summer.

Alessandro Palazzi at Dukes London doesn't shake or stir his Martinis, he uses Sacred Gin directly from the freezer and pours it into a frozen glass (to which has been added a minuscule amount of vermouth). You can buy small freezers that will fit under or behind the bar that will hold a couple of bottles of gin and vodka, some Martini glasses, and an ice bucket. If you don't have space behind or beneath the bar a big freezer in your kitchen with an ice maker would be ideal. You then need a designated drink space which you must guard zealously against encroaching ice creams, fish sticks, and the like.

SETTING UP

It's worth spending a bit of time and money on your cocktail kit rather than just ordering the cheapest thing you can find on the internet. After all, there's no point putting all that thought and care into your bar and then stinting on the accessories. The Cocktail Kingdom Essential Cocktail Set, consisting of a Boston shaker, jigger, measuring jug, bar spoon, and strainer is a great place to start. Quality tools will not only last longer but using beautiful objects—a silver-plated decanter shaped like a rocket ship, say—will turn making a simple cocktail into an event. Doing the little things really well is the essence of being a good host.

This set is called the Quench Cocktail Collection (*above*) and it was put together by Quench to go with their bespoke home bars. It includes a Japanese mixing glass, Yukiwa bar spoon, Yukiwa Japanese strainer, Yukiwa Baron shaker, fine strainer, Japanese jigger, dash bottle collection, and lots of other useful things.

Almost everything you need to make the classics (*opposite*). This basic kit includes a copper cocktail shaker, tumbler, Martini glass, jigger, strainer, measuring spoons, and ice. Simply add booze… and guests of course. Don't forget the guests.

The cocktail shaker

The first thing people buy when they get into cocktails is a shaker. For most drinks, you could just use a jug, but let's face it, if you're reading this book, you need a proper shaker. The idea of a shaker isn't just to mingle the ice with the drink but to introduce air into your cocktail, especially if you are using egg whites to create a foam.

There are two basic sorts. The first is the standard three-piece shaker consisting of the body, a strainer, and a lid. The strainer has big holes that are fine for coarse straining, but for anything finer you'll need to use a sieve or tea strainer as well. I have

a silver-plated brass one at home in that classic 1920s shape that I don't dare polish in case it takes the last of the silver plate off. Shakers can also come in aluminum, stainless steel, chrome, solid silver, glass, or plastic. They are easy to find secondhand, as they were at one time a common wedding present, though it's rare to find an intact kit. They tend not to be expensive—unless you find a totally fabulous Russel Wright shaker and cup set in aluminum with a cork wrap so your hands don't get too cold, or one by Norman Bel Geddes, designer of the revolutionary Chrysler Airflow car, whose cocktail kit looks like a skyscraper. If you're buying new, the Usagi heavyweight shaker in copper-plated stainless steel is a quality piece of kit or Oliver Bonas does a just-the-right-side-of-too-much pineapple-shaped shaker.

The other kind of shaker is known as a Boston shaker (see page 149 top right). It consists of a pint glass that fits into a metal cup. You give your cocktail a shake and then strain it from the glass using a Hawthorne strainer (see page 154). The Boston shaker looks very professional and holds more than a standard shaker. The drawback is that the two parts often get stuck together; there is a trick to separating them without covering yourself in booze.

In the 1950s fashionable ladies would not leave the house without portable cocktail kits for whipping up Martinis and Sidecars on the go (*left*). These sort of things were popular wedding presents. Nowadays complete sets are rare and can go for a lot of money at auction.

A collection of vintage silver cocktail shakers is displayed on a shelf in Alexandre Ricard's living room (*opposite*). Note that used Absolut bottles can be made into fetching lamps with just a little ingenuity. This one was created by Mathieu Mercier.

A Lillet Violet cocktail is surrounded by shakers from the 1930s, a Danish Art Deco shaker, a "Cobbler" cocktail shaker with integrated strainer and a French Saint Louis crystal and silver-plated evening cocktail shaker (*above*).

The White Negroni is made from Suze, Lillet, and gin—it was originally created by Wayne Collins during Vinexpo 2001 (*opposite*). A vintage jigger is used for measuring and a julep strainer to retain the ice cubes when serving.

A silver-plated Art Deco cocktail shaker with an integrated lemon juicer and a vintage copy of *The Savoy Cocktail Book* (1930) by Harry Craddock (*above left*). A drinks tray with silver shaker and coupe glasses with a collection of pineapple-shaped ice buckets (*above right*). Gleaming cocktail equipment consisting of ice bucket, shaker, jigger, and glasses at the famous Colony Palms Hotel in Palms Springs, California, a popular mob hangout in the 1930s (*below*).

FROSTED STAINLESS STEEL

1930S COCKTAIL SHAKER

BOSTON SHAKER

MID-CENTURY RECIPES

COPPER "COBBLER"

RIBBED CHROME

CONTEMPORARY CHROME

VINTAGE CUT GLASS

MID-CENTURY GLASS

MEASURING DEVICES

Making cocktails is an exact science; it's more like baking than cooking. You should be suspicious of bartenders who do everything by sight. It requires precision and at your home bar you can take the time to be precise. That doesn't mean you can't be generous, but it's worth measuring things carefully.

- **Shot glass or jigger** For measuring quickly, you can use a shot glass or, even better, get a jigger. Usually made of metal, this measures single shots on one side (1 fl oz/25ml) and double on the other (2 fl oz/50ml).
- **Jug** For more exact cocktail making, use a small glass measuring jug with gradations in milliliters, fluid ounces, and tablespoons.
- **Measuring spoons** For very small measures use a set of measuring spoons, or just use standard teaspoons and tablespoons.
- **Electronic scales** These are useful for measuring solids when you need exact amounts.
- **Pipettes** For adding carefully measured amounts of bitters, tinctures, etc. Also you get to feel like a scientist when using them, a bonus in my book.
- **Perfume atomizer** For spraying minute mists of vermouth, bitters, or even absinthe onto your cocktails. Perfect if you like a very Dry Martini. You can buy new ones or use vintage perfume bottles, but make sure you clean them thoroughly— you don't want your cocktail to taste of Tendre Poison or Blue Stratos.

Pouring a Pink Lady, a cocktail made from gin, lemon juice, and grenadine, all shaken together with ice and an egg white (see page 210). The perfect Pink Lady should not be too sweet, and the consistency should be as silky as expensive lingerie (*previous pages*).

A collection of the key measuring devices, including jiggers, jug, measuring spoons, and tongs for picking up pieces of ice, with shakers in the background (*left*).

MIXING

Cocktails are all about combining ingredients, usually either by shaking or stirring. This is the kit you need to mix up some magic.

- **Hawthorne strainer** A piece of metal with a spring around the edge that fits snugly into your shaker. Strains more finely than the built-in strainer in your shaker, but not as finely as a sieve. Most cocktail kits will contain one of these.
- **Stirrers** A long stick, also known as a swizzle stick, for stirring cocktails. Usually plastic but you can get wood, stainless steel, or even antique silver ones. They also come in various novelty varieties: Tiki, skulls, sexy ladies, that sort of thing.
- **Sieve or tea strainer** Useful for removing fruit seeds and those small slivers of ice that normal strainers will miss.

- **Muddler** Essentially a large piece of wood that functions as a pestle in your glass. Used for mashing up sugar cubes, mint, fruit, etc. It's hard to make a proper Mojito, Caipirinha, or Mint Julep without one.
- **Bar spoon** A very long spoon that can reach down to the bottom of the tallest highball glass. They can be in copper, stainless steel, or plastic (not so smart-looking.) If you are planning on making a lot of layered drinks, such as Irish coffee, then you should buy a bar spoon with a flat end. This makes liquids poured down the spoon spread out more easily on top of the denser liquid below.
- **Blenders** Countertop blenders first appeared in the 1930s and were the vital piece of apparatus in the evolution of the traditional Daiquiri to the modern frozen Daiquiri. The classic Waring Blender was launched in 1937 and is still going strong today. Blenders proved very popular

with customers, though less popular with jazz musicians, who complained about people ordering frozen Daiquiris during the saxophone solo. You'll need a fairly heavy-duty number, so check that it can crush ice without ruining the blades. It might also be worth getting a hand blender for roughly blitzing fruit in your shaker or a whisk attachment for making super-stiff foams.

PREPPING

The best host is the well-prepared host. Here are some often overlooked bits of equipment that will ensure that all your ingredients are ready when your guests arrive.

- **Knives** You need a small knife with a serrated blade and then a larger all-purpose kitchen knife such as a Sabatier or Wusthof. Look after your knife. You should always make sure it is razor sharp. It sounds counterintuitive, but a sharp knife is much less dangerous than a blunt one as it's less likely to slip as you use it. Don't leave your knives lying around in the sink; wash them immediately and return them to a wooden stand. I get my kitchen knives professionally sharpened once a year and then use a steel to maintain the blade. Also worth following is Kingsley Amis's advice: cut things up in advance, before you've had a double Dry Martini.
- **Cutting board** A wooden one would be fine, but a plastic cutting board with a rubberized back so it doesn't slip is really what you need.
- **Peeler** I find those plastic fruit peelers with very sharp metal blades invaluable for creating citrus peel twists (see page 250). Our fruit bowl is always full of half-naked lemons and oranges that have had the peeler treatment. With a bit of practice, it's easy to remove a piece of peel without taking

the pith with it. It's also very easy to take bits of your fingers off—be careful.
- **Grater** A fine metal grater is essential for nutmeg or a fine sprinkling of lemon zest.
- **Miscellaneous containers** If you're going to make your own sugar syrups, infusions, flavored vodkas, and so on start collecting jelly jars, old vinegar bottles, etc. If you go to professional bars you'll often see all manner of glass containers repurposed in this way. Don't forget about sealed Tupperware bowls for keeping chopped fruit, herbs, etc. fresh.

Detail of the under-bar prep space in the "Q-Series" bar from Quench Home Bars. This sort of setup would not look out of place in a professional bar (*opposite, left*).

An opportunity to see the Quench Gin Trolley in action: serving a Dry Martini from a crystal jug, using a Hawthorne strainer to keep out the ice (*opposite, right*).

It's always a good idea to cut your limes in advance when entertaining. and always use a very sharp knife (*above*). Much safer than some blunt thing that will slide around all over the place.

SERVING

Serving drinks isn't just about taste and smell, the eye is equally important. An elegant decanter or a vintage punch bowl provides a sense of occasion.

• **Jugs** A clear glass jug on the bar to keep your muddlers, bar spoons, etc. in is a good touch. It's also very handy for mixing larger quantities than will fit in your shaker, especially if it has gradations up the side (like the Yarai Jigger jug). Another thing that looks very smart is a Victorian claret jug. These are glass jugs with silver or silver-plated handles. We have one that holds two bottles of wine. It's great for serving water, but also useful for Margaritas, etc. And wine, of course.

• **Decanters** If you're serving old red wines or vintage port then you will need a decanter.

You can spend hundreds of dollars on baroque blown-glass examples that are impossible to clean, but something like the Riedel Vinum Cabernet decanter looks splendid at a more reasonable price, and it's easy to clean.

• **Punch Bowls** Punch is the forerunner of the modern cocktail. The word is usually said to derive from an Indian word, "*panch*," meaning five, though there is some debate about the etymology. The number represents the five components: alcohol, water, sour, sweet, and spice. Originally punches were drunk in colonial India to disguise the taste of arak, a potent spirit distilled from date palms. At one point there were 700 punch houses in Calcutta. The drink reached its apotheosis in the 19th century when lavish punches containing rum, cognac, fruit, and champagne would be served at parties. Charles

A good punch should be all about generosity: lots of booze, lots of fruit, and lots of ice (except not, of course, in a hot punch.) This Charlotte Rose punch in a stemmed bowl is made from wine, lemon and orange juice, and fresh strawberries (*opposite*).

A vintage soda syphon, glass with a metal mesh surround, and also known as the seltzer bottle, will look splendid on the bar. But be warned it might be hard to find carbon dioxide canisters to fit, so it might just be for show (*left*).

Dickens was a massive punch enthusiast. No upper class or middle class household would be complete without a large punch bowl in glass, earthenware, or china, with a set of matching cups.

Punches are rather out of fashion so you can pick up antique sets for not too much money. Some bowls have a place underneath where you can put a burner or candle to keep your hot punch warm. A punch, whether served hot or cold, is a communal experience; everyone drinks the same thing. A large silver punch bowl bubbling with champagne and smelling sweetly of alcohol makes a magnificent centerpiece to a party and, as you make it in advance, you have more time for socializing.

• **Soda syphon** A glass soda syphon from the 1930s with wire mesh around the bottle does look superb sitting on the bar. Just make sure that your old bottle is still airtight and will take modern CO_2 cartridges. Those vintage Schweppes ones are not easy to refill. iSi makes modern ones in both retro designs and more contemporary versions in aluminum. You should use filtered tap water, especially if you live in a hard water area, as mineral deposits will clog up your syphon. Filtered water also tastes cleaner. A soda syphon means that you don't have to open a bottle of sparkling water whenever you need a splash of soda or run the risk of putting some slightly flat water in your drink. The horror! With cartridges costing very little, it should in the long run work out cheaper than sparkling water. Resist the urge to have a Marx Brothers–esque soda syphon fight if you have more than one. Not cool.

• **Openers** A few years ago no home was complete without one of those lavish, and expensive, Screwpull corkscrews. The advantage of these is that they have a very long screw, go down the exact center of the cork, apply an even force, and have a lot of leverage. I find, though, I only use mine for removing very old corks from port bottles that I worry will crumble. For all other occasions I use a good-quality waiter's friend, one with a small blade for removing the foil, a solid Teflon-coated screw, and a double-action lever. With not very much practise, it's much the easiest way to remove almost any cork. Most wine merchants will sell you a perfectly functional opener for under $5, or you can buy fancy ones from Le Creuset or Laguiole. Don't buy the very cheapest one. Avoid anything flimsy—I'm thinking of those corkscrews with the two arms

A cut crystal decanter on the center of a dining table, holding port—just make sure you don't pass it the wrong way round the table (*above left*). A modern crystal decanter sports a rather smart silver stopper in the shape of a stag (*above right*). This would be perfect for your rare single malt Scotch. At one stage every civilized home would have had three crystal decanters: one for port, one for sherry, and one for whisky (*below*). Time to return to those days, don't you think?

Whisky on the rocks, served from a traditional decanter (*above*). A jug of Byrrh, a bitter liqueur made from quinine and sweet red wine (*below*). Contemporary glass decanters displayed on a red lacquer sideboard (*right*).

you pull down, or ones with a sharp screw like a drill bit; it will just shred the cork. Your waiter's friend will have a bottle opener, but I'm particularly partial those metal ones bartenders use to open beer with a flourish. Or, if you keep losing it, what about a vintage countertop Pepsi-Cola one?

- **Pourers** These rubber and metal devices fit into the top of bottles for easy pouring. The benefit is that the precious spirit comes out slowly and controllably, making measuring easier. You can also buy cork and metal ones that fit into smaller bottles. I keep bitters in an ornate bottle with a silver pourer. It's a joy to use.

- **Optics** For that classic saloon look, suspend bottles upside down on the back bar with an optic, so you get a standard measure. They're fun to use and you get to channel your inner landlord, but not really necessary. They look a bit miserly if you're making a drink that doesn't require exact measurement, such as a gin and tonic.

- **Drip trays, beer mats, coasters, etc.** To serve your drinks a metal drip tray or a dimpled rubber bar mat are both very handy. Add beer towels if you're going for the old-fashioned boozer look. If you have wooden furniture or anything that might be stained by moisture then drinks coasters are essential. We have colorful Portuguese earthenware tiles, which are handy for protecting furniture from both hot and cold things.

- **Linens** Something practical that completes your bar: lots of freshly laundered white dish towels. They will hold your glass or shaker steady when you're stirring, stop your chopping board sliding around, and muffle the noise of the blender and other electrical equipment. And for you, a smart bar apron. (Not one saying "Hangover under construction" please.) You can buy special bartender's aprons in canvas with leather pockets for corkscrews, etc. but any plain one will do.

CONSERVING

You never know, you might have some wine left over at the end of the night, so here are some tips for how to store open bottles so they keep their vim.

- **Champagne stoppers** Please don't put a spoon, silver or otherwise, in the top of a bottle. It doesn't do anything. If you want to keep a bottle of champagne over night (and honestly who doesn't finish the bottle in a night?) then you need a stopper, a device made from plastic, rubber, and metal that seals a sparkling wine bottle to preserve the fizz. It's perfect for keeping a bottle of Prosecco in the fridge for making spritzes.

- **Vacuvin** A small pump with a rubber stopper often used in wine bars to suck the air out of opened bottles. I have my doubt about its efficacy. In fact I sometimes find that wines that have had the Vacuvin treatment taste worse the next day, as if all the life has been sucked out of them. The best technique for preserving wine is to keep empty plastic mineral water bottles handy. Decant the wine into the bottle and squeeze so that there's no air, tighten the lid, and transfer the wine to the fridge. I've had wines that have lasted a week this way.

- **Coravin** A brilliant invention consisting of a surgical-strength thin needle attached to a trigger with a canister of inert argon gas. You push the needle through the cork (this only works with real cork) into the wine, squeeze the trigger, and a small measure of wine comes out of a spout. The wine is then replaced with the inert gas so no oxygen comes into contact with it. When you remove the needle the natural elasticity of the cork reseals the bottle. I've taken measures out of bottles using my Coravin and then tried the wine a year later and it's still been in perfect condition. You can buy replacement canisters of argon gas.

GLASSES

You could end up buying special glasses for each cocktail, wine, and even each beer, but instead I've provided an essential list and a desirable list. You really don't need that many different types. Just as the Swiss make the best watches, the finest glassware still comes from the area of Europe famous for glass blowing in the 18th and 19th century, the former Habsburg Empire, present day Austria, Czech Republic, Hungary, Slovakia, and Slovenia. The French are good for more basic stuff, with makes such as Duralex and Arc.

Essential Glasses

- **Martini glass** That classic shape! The long stem so that your hand doesn't warm your cocktail. Whatever you drink out of it tastes sophisticated, even a Cosmopolitan.
- **All-purpose wine glass** I'll let you into a little trade secret: you only need one type of wine glass. The one most of the wine trade use is called a Zalto Universal (Austrian naturally), which is a hand-blown ultra-light glass. It'll work for red, white, sherry, and even champagne. I find it a bit too delicate for me, however, so I use a Dartington red wine glass (made in Slovakia). It's short (perfect for clumsy guests who knock things over) and more robust than the Zalto. Whatever glass you buy it should have a stem, space for a good swirl without looking like a goldfish bowl, and a lip that curves in at the top to traps the aromas. This shape also works well for stronger beers, such as Belgian ales. I love the look of cut-crystal glasses, but they are useless for wine appreciation.
- **Tumbler** Also known as an Old Fashioned glass, it's a short, heavy glass. In my house we have a mixture of antique cut-crystal ones and heavy-duty Duralex ones. You can use them for almost any drinks: whisky, water, or a G&T.

- **Highball glass** Also known as a Collins glass, this is what you want for long drinks with lots of ice, such as a Campari and soda. It's fine for lager and bitter, too.
- **Sherry copita** Basically a very small white wine glass, this is one of the world's great glasses, designed so that your sherry doesn't get too warm in the Spanish sun when sharing a bottle of chilled fino. Also perfect for whisky, port, madeira, and cognac. If you're serious about spirits and fortified wines, they are essential.

An Old Fashioned cocktail in an old-fashioned hotel, on the counter of the Green Bar at the Madison Hotel in New York (*above*).

A glass of red wine, a Campari and soda, a dry white wine, a whisky on the rocks, and a Dry Martini with a lemon twist (*overleaf, from left to right*).

Desirable Glassware

- **Beer glasses** If you're serving draught beer then it's worth getting some plain straight-sided pint glasses or those dimpled jugs. If you're serving bottled beer then half pint glasses are best, or my own personal favourite, the chalice, the shape that you often get in French bars. You can also buy specialist beer-tasting glasses.
- **Spanish G&T glass** A huge bowl on a stem for making enormous Spanish-style G&Ts, heavy on the ice and gin, light on the tonic.
- **Port glass** Cut crystal makes the mellow glow of a mature port look absolutely divine and adds a sense of occasion to the table. They are surprisingly adaptable: you can serve Martinis, Brandy Sours, Gin Fizzes, etc. in them. They are not, however, that good for appreciating aroma, so if you're serious about tasting port then a sherry copita works better.
- **Champagne flute** These preserve the bubbles in the wine and also add to the sense of occasion when you get out the bubbly. However, if you're really trying to enjoy all facets of your champagne, then a good-quality white wine glass works much better.
- **Champagne coupe** A much-maligned glass, as your sparkling wine will lose its bubbles quicker than in a flute. But don't dismiss the coupes because a) they are fun to drink from b) they are versatile: Martinis, Margaritas, and Manhattans all look splendid in a coupe.
- **White wine glass** This has a smaller bowl than a red wine glass. I like the ones that are almost halfway to a flute so they can be used for sparkling and still whites as well as lighter reds. The Riedel Veritas Riesling/Zinfandel is a lovely shape.
- **Large Bordeaux and/or Burgundy glasses** I have a set of enormous Riedel Bordeaux glasses that I get out about once a year if I've got a mature Bordeaux or something similar. Beware they are very easy to break.
- **Cognac glass** Nobody, least of all in the Cognac region, uses those big brandy balloons anymore; they accentuate the alcohol too much. Instead they use something not dissimilar to a sherry copita, only with a slightly bigger bowl. This also works well for whisky appreciation.
- **Margarita glass** Looks like a big coupe with a bowl underneath it. If you're a big Margarita drinker then you need these, otherwise you could use a coupe or even a tumbler.
- **Nick & Nora glass** Named after Nick and Nora Charles, characters in the 1934 film *The Thin Man*. It looks a little like a small wine goblet and it's perfect for giving your Manhattans, Martinis, and so on a vintage look.

A collection of useful glassware: from the front counter-clockwise, a coupe, a brandy glass, a fishbowl, a champagne flute, a Bordeaux glass, a white wine glass, a tankard, and a port glass (*above*).

The same glasses looking much happier filled with the right alcoholic beverages (*opposite*).

TOP GEAR

When you've mastered the Martini and perfected your punch, it is time to put on a white coat and embrace your mad scientist side with some laboratory-grade equipment.

- **Coffee machine** You probably don't need or indeed have the space for one of these at your bar, but if you make a lot of Espresso Martinis it might be worth getting a small Nespresso machine so you don't have to keep rushing between the kitchen and the bar. This is the easiest way of making a decent espresso in the home, and if they're good enough for many Michelin-starred restaurants then they are good enough for us.
- **Still** Channel your inner alchemist with a spot of home distillation. Distillation works on the principle that alcohol evaporates at a lower temperature than water. You gently heat an alcoholic liquid, the alcohol vapor rises, leaving most of the water behind, and then you cool the alcohol vapor to turn it back into a liquid. That's the basics. It's a lot more complicated than that, as you don't just have the alcohol you want—ethanol—and water, you have all kinds of other compounds that evaporate at different temperatures, some of which are desirable in small quantities and some of which are highly toxic, such as methanol. It's worth being taught to do this properly. This is not for the faint hearted.

  You can buy little copper stills that are made in Portugal from as small as 5 pints (2.5 liters). They have gas burners underneath and look like tools used by medieval alchemists, which in a sense they are; the basic equipment for distillation hasn't changed since the middle ages. Once you have your still, you are ready to begin. You could distill your own vodka from fermented cereals, but in order to make gin most people buy neutral alcohol, essentially high-strength vodka, water it down, and then redistill it with botanicals such as juniper, cinnamon, and lemon peel (this is known as rectifying). Some people put the botanicals directly into the spirit, other suspend them in a basket above. Producing a basic gin is not that hard, but getting the recipe just right and consistent is difficult. You will probably need a license and a safety certificate, depending on where you are based and what it is exactly you are doing. Oh and not only do you run the risk of poisoning someone, but the process itself is potentially dangerous as you are heating highly flammable alcohol. Jamie Baxter from Burleighs distillery in Leicester, who runs a consultation business helping people set up their own distilleries, gave me some helpful advice: "Don't use cheap equipment. It can explode."
- **Rotary evaporator** A seriously fancy piece of laboratory kit that works by distilling liquids at low pressure, meaning that evaporation takes place at a cooler temperature. Think how water boils at a lower temperature at high altitude. This technique means that you preserve aromas that would be destroyed or altered during conventional distillation. It can be used to create infusions, concentrations and hydrosols—water-based infusions used for creating floral waters. Some quite fancy gins such as Sacred are made using

Having your bitters, vermouths, etc. in dash bottles will make preparing cocktails so much easier. This is part of the Quench Cocktail Collection (*opposite*).

this technique. You're looking at a minimum of $3,500 for a rotary evaporator.

- **Smoking** If you want to smoke your cocktails and frankly who doesn't, you'll need a smoking gun such as a PolyScience. You simply add your choice of wood such as oak, hickory, or applewood, switch it on, wait for it to heat up and a fan will blow smoke out of the gun. Much easier than trying to start a fire in your kitchen.
- **Whipped-cream dispenser** Not essential, but not expensive either—you can pick one up for $15. If you want to make your foams the professional way, you'll need one of these. It fills whatever you put in it with nitrous oxide (aka laughing gas) to create millions of tiny bubbles.
- **Sodastream** Go retrotastic by making your own sparkling drinks. These were very popular when I was growing up in the '80s; you'd mix water with a flavored syrup and then your sodastream would charge the liquid with CO_2. The problem was that the syrups plus water never tasted as good as the real thing out of a bottle. But sodastreams are undergoing a renaissance as people start making their own infusions, syrups, and soft drinks. What could be better than homemade sparkling ginger beer?
- **Ice cream maker** Cuisinart make a good countertop one. It saves you having to do all that churning by hand. You can use this to make frozen Daiquiris, wine slushies and that sort of thing. My wife makes a lovely ice cream with Portuguese Moscatel wine.
- **Centrifuge** Used in laboratory work, these machines separate liquids from solids by spinning the liquid very fast and causing the solids to fall to the bottom. They are just starting to be used by professional bartenders to create new ingredients such as clarified orange juice (it has the flavor of fresh oranges but the texture of water) or to remove solid matter from syrups and infusions. You'll need to add enzymes to help with the

separation process. Professional bartenders use big machines with space for larger liquid containers, rather than the test tubes more common in lab machines. They can cost up to $15,000, but if you are just playing around at home you can buy something like a Ample Scientific Champion E-33 for $200.

- **Portable induction hob** If you make a lot of hot drinks, such as toddies or rum punches, then an induction hob is a very safe way of keeping things warm on your bar. It only works with ferrous cooking equipment.
- **Sous-vide machine** This darling of the molecular gastronomy movement slowly cooks things sealed in a plastic bag in a basin of hot but not boiling water. Yes—it's essentially fancy boil-in-the-bag cookery. The idea is that the slow cooking makes meat meltingly tender. It is now used by bartenders to create syrups and infusions such as chili vodka quickly, but without heating your liquid too much, which could cook the flavors and worse still lose alcohol. It's especially useful for finishing off barrel-aged cocktails (see page 170) as it mimics the process used in the production of Noilly Prat vermouth and Madeira wine, which are gently heated to smooth out flavors. You can buy sous-vide machines with a built-in basin like miniature versions of restaurant machines from companies such as Magimix. Alternatively, immersion circulators like the Anova Precision Cooker Wifi work by keeping a pan of water at a constant temperature, and they can be controled from your smartphone.

Your bar can be a laboratory, too (*opposite*). A Suze tonic in a highball glass sits in front of a collection of vintage conical flasks and measuring tubes on a wooden table.

BARREL-AGING

You may have noticed that many bars nowadays have a small barrel on the bar from which they dispense cocktails. Aging of cocktails was a trend pioneered by bartenders such as Jeffrey Morgenthaler from Oregon. For some this is a hipster step too far, but having tried many such cocktails I can confirm that wood-aging can do something magical. It rounds off sharp edges: the three different components in a Negroni, for example, become more integrated and it takes on a distinct nuttiness, like a tawny port or an oloroso sherry. Experimenting with wood-aging in your home can be tremendously satisfying, as you have the chance to taste your liquid to see how it is developing. It makes one feel like a winemaker or a master whisky blender.

Originally barrels were just used as containers. They were watertight, relatively cheap to produce and more durable than the amphora (clay jars) that the Romans used. You wouldn't want to roll out the amphora, it would break. Wine or spirits would be shipped in barrels and on long journeys it was found that the contents had changed, sometimes for the worse (a dirty barrel might turn your claret to vinegar), but often for the better. Rum shipped over from the Caribbean would be transformed from a clear pungent spirit into something darker and smoother. And the longer it spent in the barrel, the darker and smoother it became. On the six-month journey through the tropics to India, Madeira wine, from an island off the coast of west Africa, changed from a highly acidic white wine into a mellow, nutty drink that became much prized by connoisseurs. Madeira just seems to get better the longer you keep it. I've had wines from the mid-19th century that tasted a bit young. Some of these wines will have spent 100 years in wood before being bottled.

Wood-aging works in a number of ways. Firstly, some of the character of the charred wood (during the barrel-making process the wooden staves are heated so that they bend) leaches into the contents of the barrel. Flavors such as cloves, vanilla, chocolate, and coffee, commonly found in wines and whiskies, come directly from the wood. Tannins, which cause that drying sensation in the mouth, also come from the wood. These flavors are most pronounced in new barrels. In older barrels—and most barrels would be used over and over again—the flavor comes from the gentle action of oxygen on the wine. Unlike glass, wood lets in a small amount of air. That gentle oxidative effect gives wines such as sherry and vermouth their distinctive nutty flavor. At Noilly Prat in the south of France they age their vermouth out in the sun to speed up the process and gently cook the wine. Finally, the previous contents of the barrel can flavor the liquid. Scotch whisky gets some of its characteristic taste from being kept in old sherry barrels. Again, this would have been discovered accidentally. As sherry was traditionally shipped in barrels, the Scots, keen sherry drinkers, would have had lots of empty barrels lying around, perfect for storing the whisky they produced.

So, with home aging, you need to think about what you want from your barrel. You can buy new barrels made from American oak relatively cheaply. These will give a powerful oaky flavor. You can buy kits that contain a barrel and a white spirit, which you age at home to create your own bourbon-style whiskey. The aging process is quicker in smaller casks because they have a greater wood-to-liquid ratio. If you don't want these strong oak flavors then you need to season the wood. This can be done by keeping the cask full of water for two months. The wood may need further seasoning, so perhaps for your first batch don't use your best

fortified wine; a reasonable quality robust red wine would be the thing or perhaps a cheaper port or sherry. Remember that whatever you season it with will seep into the wood and some of that flavor will come out in your drink. Or you could buy pre-used barrels, which have the advantage of being ready-seasoned, but they will need a really good clean. You can get anything from a little 2 pint (1 liter) one with a tap that sits on the bar to a 60 gallon (225 liter) ex-Bordeaux barrel to keep in your cellar.

Having your own cask is particularly popular in Australia, where companies will sell you wood barrels with some fortified port-style wine to put in them. After six months or so in the cask, try the wine and then top it up with something similar. It's important that you keep the barrel topped up or the wine will oxidize. Keep tasting and topping up every few months and your fortified wine should start to develop a fantastic taste, with the nutty complexity of old wines perfectly mingled with

the fruit of the young. Congratulations, you have created a rudimentary solera, a system for blending sherry in Spain that is also used in Italy, Portugal, and Australia. You can do a similar thing with spirits such as whisky, rum, or brandy, but you don't need to be quite so slavish in topping up the barrel.

With a properly seasoned cask, you're ready to start making your own cocktails or infusions, or you could experiment with making your own vermouth or amaro. One of my most memorable drinking experiences was at a bed and breakfast in Pauillac where the owner made his own concoctions from Martinique rum and juice from local merlot grapes aged with cinnamon and other spices. On a hot evening in the vineyards it tasted delicious.

Aging cocktails might sound like trendy nonsense, but time in wood with oxygen contact smooths out the edges and adds complexity to drinks such as the Negroni (*above*).

THE WELL-STOCKED BAR

You don't need hundreds of bottles to make the classics: gin, whiskey, bitters, and vermouth will get you a long way. But the joy of having your own bar is you have the space to let your collection expand.

I have arranged this section in decreasing order of importance for the home bartender. You could stock your bar with items just from the first two sections and still put on a damn good if rather rowdy party.

1

SPIRITS

Hard liquor is the backbone of the cocktail

2

AMARI AND BITTERS

These provide a supporting role, adding complexity to your drink

3

LIQUEURS

Spirits flavored with whatever you fancy: spices, herbs, or fruit

4

FORTIFIED WINES

Wines strengthened with brandy, delicious in cocktails or on their own

5

SPARKLING WINES

Not just champagne, but Prosecco, Cava and other sparkling wines

6

TABLE WINES

A brief guide to storing and serving wine

7

BEER

From the lightest most refreshing pilsner to an oak-aged imperial stout

8

NON-ALCOHOLIC ESSENTIALS

Don't skimp on the quality of your mixers and garnishes

Truly this is a well-stocked bar, with a superb array of whiskies, vermouths, bitters, and liqueurs (***previous pages***). The look is very trendy, with bare brick, polished copper piping, vintage exposed lightbulbs and an enormous metal sign saying "BAR" as a handy reminder, should you need it.

With its wood paneling, globe lamps, and tasteful minimalist bar stools this contemporary home bar owes more than a little to mid-century style (***opposite***). The bar displays bottles on open shelves within a built-in wall-to-wall cabinet.

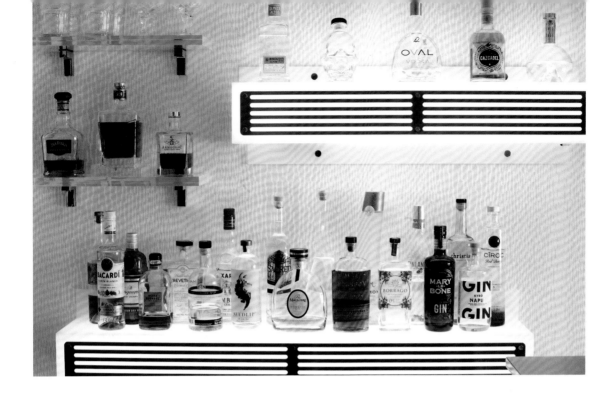

SPIRITS

Before I dive into the wondrous world of spirits, it's helpful to know a little about how they are made. Distillation works on the principle that alcohol evaporates at a lower temperature than water. So, by the careful application of heat, you can separate alcohol from water. You don't, however, just get two compounds: there are all kinds of other things given off which in small quantities can be desirable. Then there are others, such as methanol, that are highly toxic. People die every year from badly distilled hooch. The art of distillation is to create a smooth, high-alcohol spirit that on one hand doesn't contain anything poisonous, but on the other isn't so pure that it tastes of nothing.

Traditionally, spirits were made in what is known as a pot still. This is a metal, usually copper, pot. You put your wine or other fermented liquid in, heat it and alcohol-rich vapors rise to the top, where they are condensed. This normally gives a spirit of about 20% proof, which is known as a low wine. Repeat the process and you end up with something of around 60–70% alcohol. The advantage of this system is that much of the character of the base liquid is preserved. The drawbacks are that it is a laborious process; spirits can only be made in batches, and it requires a high degree of skill to avoid any nastiness.

The invention of the column still by, among others, Aeneas Coffey changed everything. In a Coffey still the liquid is pumped in continuously and the spirit is drawn off at the top. The taller the still, the stronger the spirit.

There's a certain amount of snobbery around pot stills versus column stills, but what matters more is the distiller's intent. You can make flavorful spirits in a column still, as they do in the Armagnac region, and bland liquids do come out of pot stills. So, as with everything in drink, let your senses be your guide and don't obsess about the distillation.

GIN

Gin is *the* most important spirit in your armory. The majority of cocktails in Harry Craddock's legendary *The Savoy Cocktail Book* (1930) are gin-based. The greatest cocktail of all, the Martini, is essentially very cold gin flavored with vermouth. But which gin should one use?

It used to be so simple: for most of us it was a choice between Gordon's and Beefeater or, for those in the know, Tanqueray. Now new brands appear every month. As a drinks writer I get more press releases about gin than any other drink. How do you pick your way through this juniper-laden minefield?

First, some basics. Gin is essentially flavored vodka. In the European Union it has to be made from high-strength neutral grain alcohol (minimum 96%) which has no flavor. In order to be classed as gin the dominant flavor has to be juniper—a berry that grows wild all over Europe—though some modern gins barely taste of juniper at all. Other flavors (known as botanicals) might include lemon, cinnamon, or licorice. I've even had a chocolate gin. It wasn't very good.

There are various ways of getting flavor into the spirit. The most common is to redistill the watered-down spirit with the botanicals, either in the liquid or in a basket above for a more subtle flavor. Then there are gins, such as Sacred in London, that are distilled using vacuum distillation so the spirit is barely heated. The final method, cold compounding, is where essential oils are added to the spirit. In the cheapest gins these flavors might be artificial. London Dry Gin does not have to come from London: it just has to be unsweetened and be made from natural ingredients.

Illuminated back shelving can lend an extra wow factor to a home bar installation. Featured here is the "Litebar" shelf by Quench Home Bars, holding an impressive selection of spirits (*opposite*).

A fusion of natural and modern materials, this specially designed drinks trolley, also by Quench, brings together high-gloss laminated birch ply with diamond-polished acrylic (*right*). The edges of the plywood are left exposed and then laquered to create a beautiful divide between the two materials.

In the US and other markets, producers don't have to use high-strength neutral grain spirit. They can use lower strength spirits as a base, which tend to have more flavor. As you'd expect from the land of the free, Americans have more freedom when it comes to their base spirit, so their gins often have a thicker texture and a pronounced cereal note, almost like an unaged whiskey. I'm very partial to Bluecoat gin and Brooklyn gin from New York.

This new world of gin is very exciting, but there is a problem for the unwary cocktailer: gin is a very broad church. Some new gins, rather than tasting strongly of juniper, might lead with cucumber, lemon, or cinnamon, which means you have to be careful when mixing your drinks. The three great tests of a gin are the Martini, the G&T and the Negroni. Whereas a traditional gin such as Beefeater works in all, newer gins often excel at one, but not the others. For example, I find a very lemony gin doesn't work in a Martini, but can be

good in a G&T. But floral gins, while lovely in a Martini, can be overpowered by tonic water. And I once had a licorice-heavy gin that did horrible things when mixed with Campari and Martini Rosso. Not nice! So by all means go mad exploring yuzu and barrel-aged gins, but for bar room basics make sure you've got a bottle of Beefeater handy, or one of the newer brands: Sipsmith, Sacred, and William Chase are all very reliable.

Finally, there's Old Tom gin. This style is a throwback to when gin was heavily sweetened to disguise the taste of the rough base spirit. When cheap high-quality grain spirit became available with the invention of the Coffey still, gin gradually became drier and drier until it became something like London dry gin. Most manufacturers carried on making a sweet gin, known as Old Tom. This style nearly died out but has now been revived and is essential for making some classic 19th-century cocktails such as the Martinez.

VODKA

Vodka might not get the spirit aficionados hot under the collar, but at some point if you entertain someone is going to ask for a vodka-based drink. Vodka is useful for adding alcohol to fruit juice, etc. If you're going to do this then you need a clean vodka of at least 40% proof, such as Absolut. You're really looking for an absence of flavor. Even (or rather especially) the very expensive vodkas trade on how little flavor they have. All the fuss about filtering and triple, quadruple, or (in the case of Ciroc) quintuple distillation is designed to make them as smooth, meaning bland, as possible.

But there's much more to vodka than a convenient vehicle for alcohol. They're a tiny percentage of the market but there are some vodkas out there offering something different. Vestal makes Polish vodkas from individual potato varieties, just as with grapes. Another Polish vodka,

Konik's Tail, is made from spelt, wheat, and rye, and bartenders rave about Aylesbury Ruck from the 86 Company in the US The key is letting the quality of the raw material shine, so there's no heavy filtering or triple distillation. These are gastronomic drinks designed for sipping with cold meats and pickles rather than knocking back ice cold. A spirit with some weight and flavor will take your vodka Martini to a whole new level of deliciousness.

So with vodka it's worth having a bottle of Absolut in the freezer for making Sea Breezes and the like, and then a bottle of something special for when your Polish mates come round.

Vodka bottles often come in a bewildering array of shapes and sizes (*above*). The bottle in the foreground is Crystal Head Vodka. It is made in Canada and the company was founded by the actor Dan Aykroyd. Its sinister charm is accentuated by backlit shelving.

AMERICAN WHISKEY

Vying with gin as the king of the cocktail counter is good old-fashioned American whiskey (usually spelled with an e in America as well as Ireland). The Manhattan, the Brooklyn, and the Old Fashioned all require the sweetness and body provided by corn (maize). Scotch or Irish just won't cut it.

For most of us this means reaching for the bourbon bottle. Bourbon is a place—Bourbon County, Kentucky—but bourbon is also a style. It can come from anywhere in the US. Bourbon by law has to be at least 51 percent corn. The remainder can be rye, which is more spicy and savory, or wheat, which is smooth and sweet. The resulting whiskey must then be aged in new charred-oak barrels.

But there's much more to American whiskey than bourbon. The other classic native style is rye, which as its name suggests is mainly made from rye, and usually corn and wheat, too. It tends to be leaner and spicier than bourbon, but still with a full body and a sweetness to it. Rye whiskey almost died out when America went vodka crazy in the '70s and '80s, but it is now back with a vengeance. In fact, American whiskey in all its forms has undergone a renaissance. Not only are bourbons and ryes more exciting than ever, but America now produces Scottish and Irish-style whiskies made mainly or wholly from malted barley. These tend to be fuller and sweeter than their old world cousins.

There's so much to try, but to make the classic cocktails you really only need one whiskey to start with. Connoisseurs tend to prefer rye in drinks such as the Manhattan, but I find bourbon with a high rye content works just as well. I'm a big fan of the High West Rendezvous Rye; Sazerac and Rittenhouse Rye are the big names among US bartenders. The Canadians, long famous for their rather anodyne whiskies, such as Canadian Club, are now making spicy rye whiskies a speciality.

For bourbon, Four Roses Small Batch has a nice combination of sweetness and spice and makes a mean Manhattan. For sipping or Mint Juleps, I can't get enough of Blanton's Original Single Barrel Bourbon. It's the one with the little metal horse on the stopper—a reminder that Kentucky is as famous for its horses as its whiskey.

SCOTCH WHISKY

There are a few cocktails, such as the Rob Roy, which specify Scotch whisky, but for me Scotch is mainly for drinking neat, with a little ice or water, or perhaps ginger beer. A well-stocked bar should include at least two Scotch whiskies: a single malt and a good everyday blend.

Most Scotches are blends of single malts, spirits made only from malted barley from one distillery and distilled in a traditional pot still, and cheaper lighter grain whiskies, made from other cereals—usually unmalted barley, wheat, rye, and maize—and distilled in a Coffey still. These blends were invented in the 19th century to appeal to the English market, who it was thought would have found neat Talisker, etc. much too challenging.

Do not turn your nose up at them. I love blended whiskies—the big brands tend to be of consistently high quality. My favorites include the rich Johnnie Walker Black Label, perfect for sipping with a little ice, and its brother the smoky robust Red Label, which is great in a long drink with ice, soda, and orange bitters. You can also buy boutique blends made in small batches by companies such as Compass Box, which are every bit as interesting as the fanciest single malts.

As for single malts, well it's hard to do the topic justice, but every home should have at least one for when an old friend comes over who you haven't seen for years. I'm particularly partial to the rich heavily sherried style from Glenfarclas (try the 15- year-old), but wouldn't turn my nose up at

In the past ten years the world has woken up to the magic of Japanese whisky, with prices growing accordingly. This selection includes a bottle of ultra-rare Hibiki 17-year-old (*above*).

a peaty Lagavulin 16-year-old. Smoky scotches are also useful for adding another layer of flavor to whiskey-based cocktails, such as an Old Fashioned or a Manhattan.

IRISH WHISKEY

A great friend neat or mixed, some brands, Jameson's especially, have an almost bourbon-like sweetness, which makes them great in cocktails. Try making a heretical Mint Julep with Bushmills Black Bush. But the real glory of Irish whiskey is their pot still whiskies. Like single malt scotch, these are distilled in a traditional still but from a mixture of malted and unmalted barley, and usually distilled three times rather than twice, as is normal in Scotland. The result is an amazing creamy texture and spicy character that is like nothing else. Most Irish whiskies are blends, with some pot still spirit, but look for all-pot still releases such as Redbreast 12-year-old or Green Spot, or ones with a high pot still content, such as Powers Gold Label 12-year-old reserve, which is good enough to make a Scotsman weep.

OTHER WHISKIES

Whisky has truly gone global in the past few years with countries such as Taiwan (I can recommend Kavalan), India (Amrut), and even England (Cotswold Distillery) now making superb spirits. It is Japan, though, which is now firmly established as a whisky superpower. The Japanese modeled their whisky industry on Scotch, but some aficionados think that the pupil may now have eclipsed the teacher. Such is the demand for Japanese whisky that most producers now release whiskies without an age statement (as they do in Scotland, too). There's just not enough aged whisky to go around. As such, it is never going to be cheap, but something like the Nikka From the Barrel 51.4% blended whisky is a great place to start.

RUM

Rum can be made either from molasses, a byproduct of sugar refining, or from juice from the sugar cane directly. The French divide the two categories into "*rhum industriale*" and "*rhum agricole.*" Most rum from the French-speaking Caribbean is *agricole* whereas most rums from English and Spanish-speaking areas are *industriale*, but don't let the word put you off. They don't taste industrial.

The spirit can be sold either unaged as white rum, or aged in oak barrels, often used bourbon casks, like whisky. The brand leader for white rum is Bacardi, through the connoisseur's choice is Wray & Nephew from Jamaica at a fearsome 63%. It certainly provides a kick to rum punches, daiquiris, etc. You can buy extremely expensive old aged rums, but for most purposes something like Appleton Estate 12-year-old from Jamaica is excellent. Bacardi 8-year-old is good, too, or try my personal favorite: Mount Gay XO from Barbados, which has something of a good cognac about it. All three are delicious sipped neat with a little ice or will make seriously classy Rum Sours.

The final category is dark rum, a blend mixed with molasses, which gives it that characteristic colour and sweetness. Myers's Original Dark Rum or Lamb's Navy are not exactly subtle, but mixed with Coca-Cola and lots of lime they are delicious.

White rum is fine, but even the most fruit-heavy cocktail will benefit from a little aged-rum magic. If you've only got room for one bottle in your drinks cabinet then I'd recommend a lightly aged rum, Mount Gay Eclipse. It's good enough to sip neat, but light and cheap enough to go into a fruit drink.

CACHAÇA

This is a pungent, unaged Brazilian rum made from sugar cane juice rather than molasses. It's something of an acquired taste on its own, but provides the essential punchiness to a Caipirinha.

BRANDY

Brandy doesn't attract the excitement that surrounds rum, gin, or whisky. Cognac, the brandy from the Charente region in western France, has a peculiar image, seen either as a drink for old men or something to be knocked back in displays of conspicuous consumption in nightclubs. This is a shame because it is a noble drink. A smooth, elegant, aged spirit, it was the model for blended whisky in the 19th century. As the world's most prestigious brandy, cognac is never going to be cheap, but if you sidestep the bling bottles aimed at Russian businessmen, you can find high quality at a surprisingly reasonable price. Delamain XO is delicate and floral, the vintages released from Frapin are superb and for mixing Hine VSOP can't be beaten. In fact, cognac is the original mixer: the cocktail of New Orleans, a Sazerac was originally made with brandy rather than bourbon. Bache-Gabrielsen makes an American oak-aged cognac that is like a cross between a bourbon and a brandy. The age indicators are worth memorizing: VS (very special) equals a minimum of two years aging, VSOP (very special old pale) is a minimum of three years, XO and Hors d'Age are a minimum of six years in cask.

Cognac isn't the only French brandy of note. From a little further south, there's armagnac. Often dismissed as cognac's country cousin, there is indeed something endearingly rustic about the way this product is made. Many armagnac producers are farmers who also make wine, keep cattle and grow tobacco. Whereas cognac is distilled twice in a pot still like malt whisky, armagnac is distilled once in a column still. But these aren't the enormous columns of grain whisky distilleries that turn out high-strength alcohol. Armagnac stills, which are often wood-fired rustic contraptions, produce a spirit of between 50 and 60% that is full of flavor. Young armagnac tends to be peppery and spicy. After long aging it takes on flavors of dried apricots and nuts known as "*rancio*"; very old armagnac tastes a lot like Speyside scotch whisky. Armagnac is drastically underpriced, which is great news for us, if not for the producers. You can buy 40-year-old brandies for around $130 a bottle. There aren't really any global brands: Delord has probably the biggest presence in the US, Baron de Sigognac occupies the same position in Britain. Both are excellent across the range, from VSOP up to rare vintage wines. After a large Gascon meal (this part of France is the home of foie gras), there's nothing better than a large glass of armagnac. They say it burns a hole in your stomach to make room for more feasting.

Cognac and armagnac are the big two, but you can find quality grape brandies from California, South Africa and Australia. The Spanish are very keen on their Brandy de Jerez, which is aged in old sweet sherry barrels and tastes like a cross between cognac and sweet oloroso sherry. Lepanto is my favorite brand. But the best non-French brandy I've ever had is Armenian—an Ararat Nairi 20-year-old. You can normally find it in airport duty-free shops.

PISCO

An unaged grape brandy from Chile and Peru, this is usually drunk in the form of a Pisco Sour.

APPLE BRANDY

Calvados, the Normandy apple brandy, can hit the heights of armagnac or cognac. It tends to be fiery and a little funky. Of the bigger brands Boulard Grand Solage is good, or try Victor Gontier for something a little more farmhouse. Laird's of New Jersey in the US produces apple brandies and Applejack, a blend of apple brandy and grain spirit. In England the Somerset Cider Brandy Company makes an English answer to calvados.

TEQUILA

This is one of those drinks that people drink too much of when young, and that puts them off for life. But there is much more to tequila than slammers. It is made (mainly) from agave cactus in Jalisco, Mexico, near the town of Tequila, hence the name. Like rum it can be drunk young or aged a little (known as Reposado) or for longer (Añejo). Cheaper brands may also contain neutral grain alcohol as well as agave spirit so look for 100 percent agave on the label. Of the bigger brands, Patrón is reliable or, of the smaller makes, Tapatio Blanco is very highly regarded among bartenders.

MEZCAL

A helpful way to think about mezcal is that it has the same relationship to tequila as armagnac does to cognac. Both Mexican spirits are made from agave, but whereas tequila has gone global, mezcal is on the whole made in old-fashioned ways by small producers. Mezcal can be made all over Mexico, whereas tequila comes from one particular area. Mezcal tends to have a smoky flavor, as the agave is cooked over hot coals before fermentation and distillation. And no it doesn't usually have a worm in the bottom. That was just a gimmick for tourists. Just as with armagnac, there aren't any really big brands, but the Del Maguey Vida, with its distinctive label by artist Ken Price, tends to be quite easy to find. Bartenders who like mezcal tend to be evangelical about it.

The traditional way to drink mezcal is neat with a slice of orange and some "*sal de gusano*" on the side (**above**). This literally means "worm salt," and consists of salt, powdered chili peppers, and crushed dried agave worms. It tastes a lot nicer than it sounds.

AMARI AND BITTERS

CAMPARI

For me Campari is the nectar of the gods, but some people hate it. It's the bitterness that inspires this strong reaction. That bitter taste is our body's way of saying, hang on a moment, are you quite sure you should be swallowing this? We are going against our instinct, but that bitterness also stimulates the appetite. Our body reacts by producing saliva and stomach acid, which is why bitter drinks make good aperitifs. The Italians have a whole range of drinks knowns as amari (meaning bitter), of which Campari is the most famous.

Campari is made in Milan from a secret mixture of herbs and spices (just like KFC), sugar, and alcohol. It used to get its red color from cochineal, but sadly no more (bottles of Campari made from real beetles are now highly prized among cocktail geeks). I find Campari's combination of sweetness and bitterness completely addictive. It's an essential ingredient in the Negroni and the Americano. It's delicious with soda water, and it's a great way of perking up a mediocre white, rosé, or fizz. No home should be without it.

Once you get a taste for bitterness there's a whole world of amari out there, including Fernet Branca, probably the bitterest thing on the planet, and Aperol, which is the opposite, tasting sweetly of oranges with only a hint of bitter. Martini Riserva Speciale Bitter is a sort of halfway house between Campari and Aperol; Cynar gets its flavor from artichokes; Picon Amer from France tastes like overcooked marmalade; and, finally, for an English take on an Italian classic, try Sacred Rosehip Cup.

VERMOUTH

You'll need two bottles of vermouth, a sweet and a dry, also known as Italian and French. The Italian stuff is a vital ingredient in the Manhattan and the French in the Martini. Vermouth is a fortified wine flavored with herbs, spices, and fruit, but the crucial ingredient in vermouth that gives it that distinct bitter edge is wormwood; the word vermouth comes from the German "*Wermut*." The best vermouths share certain taste similarities and production techniques with good fortified wines. For example, Noilly Prat is aged in the heat like Madeira, and some of the richer types of sweet vermouth have a distinctly porty taste.

For most of us the go-to vermouths are Martini Rosso for sweet and Noilly Prat for dry. Both are good products; Noilly Prat in particular is superb. Just to confuse matters, Martini makes an French-style vermouth called Extra Dry, which is a bit dull, and Noilly Prat makes an excellent Italian-style vermouth that is very hard to find. There are numerous other choices, which can be divided into the old guard and the new wave. The Italian old guard includes Punt e Mes, which is very bitter, Carpano Antica Formula, Cocchi, or, my own favourite, Cinzano 1757 Rosso, a rich premium version of standard Cinzano. In the French camp there's Dolin, light and aromatic, and Lillet Blanc, made from Bordeaux grapes. But now there are also vermouths made all over the world, some of which take their wine base very seriously indeed, such as Asterley Bros vermouth, based on Kentish Pinot Noir, and Regal Rogue, based on Australian Sauvignon Blanc. The sherry giant González-Byass make some excellent Spanish vermouths.

Vermouth provides magic when paired with other complex drinks such as gin, Campari, or whisky, but it also tastes great on its own. With its combination of wine, spirits, herbs, fruit, and spices, think of it as a ready-made cocktail.

AROMATIZED WINES

These are very similar to vermouth, but without the wormwood. Classics include Dubonnet, flavored with cinchona bark like tonic water, or Byrrh, another cinchona-based spirit but made from a port-style wine in the south of France. Then there are Cocchi Americano from Italy and Lillet from France, both flavored with gentian root. All of these serve a similar purpose to vermouth, being excellent neat, mixed with gin or used in cocktails.

BITTERS

Bitters were originally marketed as medicine. The most famous brand Angostura, named after a town in Trinidad, was invented by a German, Johann Siegert, as a seasickness remedy, which may be why it was popularized by the Royal Navy, who mixed it with Plymouth gin to make a pink gin.

No well-stocked bar should be without a bottle of Campari (*opposite*). It's a very versatile mixer, but finds its apotheosis when mixed with gin and Italian vermouth in the mighty Negroni.

Peychaud's bitters is essential for creating the cocktail of New Orleans, the Sazerac (*right*). It was invented in 1830 by an apothecary, Antoine Amédée Peychaud. It is now made by the company that makes Sazerac rye.

Sold in tiny bottles so often overlooked, bitters are your secret weapon for making delicious drinks. An Old Fashioned wouldn't be an Old Fashioned without that strange distinctive taste of Angostura, and a couple of drops of bitters turns a glass of sparkling water with lime into a grown-ups' drink.

Angostura is made from a cocktail of aromatic barks, herbs, and fruit and is the most famous brand, but there are other types. I am very partial to orange bitters (Fee Brothers and Angostura make versions). It's particularly wonderful for pepping up a whisky and soda. In fact, a good way to think of bitters is as the salt and pepper of the cocktail cabinet, finishing off, bringing out flavors, sharpening things up. The final one you need is Peychaud's, native to New Orleans.

If you really get the bitters bug you can start making your own (see page 248).

LIQUEURS

Liqueurs are alcohol flavored with something. It could be fruit, herbs, spices, or even vegetables. There are more liqueurs out there than you can shake a stick at. Every holiday destination has a native liqueur to sell to tourists, who put it at the back of the cupboard when they get home, never to be drunk. Here are a few that won't gather dust behind your bar.

ANISEED SPIRITS

There are few countries in Europe and the near east that don't have an aniseed-based spirit. Though I've lumped them in one category they are very different. The daddy is absinthe, illegal in some countries due to the toxic properties of one of the principal ingredients, wormwood. Nowadays commercial absinthe from Switzerland or the Czech Republic will have minuscule quantities of wormwood, so don't worry. Some bartenders like to rinse a glass in it to jazz up classic cocktails such as the Tuxedo (very similar to a Martini, made with sherry instead of vermouth.)

Or one can use pastis, such as Ricard, which is essentially absinthe without the wormwood. A glass of pastis is also delicious on a summer's day with ice and water. Also fitting into the summer sipper category is arak from Lebanon, which is made from grape brandy flavored with aniseed. It's especially good with mezze, as that crisp taste cleans the palate between dishes. Ouzo from Greece and raki from Turkey serve a similar purpose, though they don't tend to be as fine as the Lebanese product. The aniseed spirits from southern Europe, including sambuca from Italy or anisette from Spain, are much sweeter; both are delicious served with an espresso on the side.

ORANGE LIQUEURS

The French have triple sec, such as Cointreau; the Dutch have orange curaçao from Bols or De Kuyper. Most are made from oranges steeped in neutral alcohol, but for a richer flavor try Grand Marnier, which is made with cognac. Triple sec is a key ingredient in the Margarita and the Sidecar.

MARASCHINO LIQUEURS

The leading brand is made by Luxardo. It's made from bittersweet Italian cherries and has an excellent almond-like quality to go alongside the sweetness. You'll need a bottle to make a Brooklyn and the Aviator, but it also adds depth and interest to cocktails such as the Old Fashioned.

FRUIT BRANDIES

You can buy fruit brandies like Slivovitz, which are distilled directly from fruit—plums in this case—but for cocktail purposes most fruit brandies are made by steeping the fruit in question in grape alcohol. They are technically liqueurs. De Kuyper from the Netherlands is the leading brand.

HERBAL LIQUEURS

The big names here are Benedictine and Chartreuse, both made by different orders of monks in France, Benedictines (obviously) and Carthusians. Chartreuse comes in two types, the sweet and comparatively mild (40%) yellow, which gets its colour from saffron, and the mighty 55% green Chartreuse, a drink so green they named a color after it. It is made from a secret blend of more than 130 herbs that has been used by the monks since the 18th century. It was in the 20th century, however, that it achieved cult status as the inspiration for writers from Evelyn Waugh to Tom Waits. It's excellent as a digestif or a cocktail ingredient and provides the ultimate *après ski* drink when mixed with coffee. Benedictine is milder and made with honey, and it features in quite a few cocktails, including the Bobby Burns, Singapore Sling, and the Vieux Carré.

SLOE GIN

This is made from gin steeped with sloes (a kind of tiny wild plum) and sugar. It's a popular pastime in Britain to go sloe picking in the Fall and make your own, but you can buy ready-made ones from Sipsmith and others. It has a porty sort of taste which works well in cocktails, or you can use it instead of cassis for an English take on a Kir.

CREME DE CASSIS, CREME DE FRAMBOISE, AND CREME DE MURE

Blackcurrant, raspberry, and blackberry liqueurs respectively, they are lovely mixed with wine, still or sparkling, or used in cocktails such as the Bramble.

AMARETTO

Very sweet almond-flavored liqueur, though the leading brand Disaronno actually gets its flavor from apricot seeds rather than almonds, so you can drink this if you have a nut allergy. Popular on the rocks as an after-dinner drink, it's even better as a sour with lots of lime juice to cut the sweetness.

COFFEE LIQUEURS

Tia Maria and Kahlua are the best-known brands. Kahlua has the edge on flavor, as it's made with rum rather than neutral alcohol. If you want to be like the dude in *The Big Lebowski* (1998), with his White Russians, you need some of this.

A selection of branded liqueurs, including a bottle of a bartender's secret weapon, Luxardo Maraschino, made from bittersweet Italian cherries (*opposite*).

Copper pendant lights illuminate Alexandre Ricard's home bar, which comprises a curved marble base and a traditional zinc counter, against a backdrop of rare bottles to get any drink aficionado drooling (*overleaf*).

FORTIFIED WINES

PORT

Port is the ultimate cold weather drink, taking the baking heat of the Douro Valley, Portugal, adding brandy to it and then bottling it to provide warmth and comfort to northerners. No wonder it is so strongly associated with Christmas. But I think port should be more than just a once a year treat. It comes in many different forms that can be sipped when the weather is cold, but also drunk chilled or used as an ingredient in cocktails and mixed drinks. It's a very versatile wine.

Port is usually made by adding brandy to still-fermenting red grapes to kill the yeasts so that you have a sweet liquid fiery with plenty of tannin. The cheapest ports are sold after a year or two in barrel to soften that fiery edge. It is, however, when you keep good port for longer that the magic happens. This can be done in two ways: it can be aged in bottle or in wooden casks. The British traditionally drank vintage port, only made in the best years, bottled young, and then kept for 20 years minimum, when it transformed into something mellow and sweetly spicy. Most people don't have the patience or indeed the cellar for such things, so you can buy ready-aged ports with some of this character, Late Bottled Vintages (LBVs), or cheaper ports from a single year that don't need so long in bottle (usually these come from a single vineyard or Quinta.) In Porto, however, they drink tawny ports, wines aged for years in cask where they slowly interact with the oxygen and the wood (see Barrel-aging, pages 170–1). They are then sold ready to drink, either with an age statement, such as 10 years or 20 years, or a vintage, when they become known as Colheitas. For me these wood-aged wines are the glory of port for the everyday drinker. They are pale in color, nutty, and respond well to chilling. A dash of tawny port works wonders in a Negroni.

Finally there is white port, which is more like a sweeter version of fino sherry. It can be a very simple drink, delicious when mixed with tonic and ice, or in rare cases have the complexity of a tawny.

Most port from the big, usually British, names, is of very high quality. Taylor's 10 Year Old Tawny is a regular in our house. If you pick up a taste for Colheitas, some of the lesser-known names— Niepoort, Kopke, and Cálem—release old vintages. Of the bottle-aged stuff, Fonseca LBV is usually excellent, especially if you can find an old bottle. Churchill's is also impeccable; in some years you'd mistake it for a vintage port. If you pick up a taste for vintage port you can buy old bottles from wine merchants for about $70.

My advice to you would be to drink more port. I adore the stuff and have to stop myself drinking it too quickly. For the moderate sipper, port is ideal as a bottle of tawny should last a month in the fridge. Just have a little glass after dinner and I promise you'll be happier.

SHERRY

The wine trade loves sherry, but for many it is something of an acquired taste. One wine merchant told me that for most of his customers sherry has "the wrong flavor. It's not fresh and fruity. It's about as far from pinot grigio as you can get."

Broadly speaking there are three types of sherry: the white, the brown and the extremely sweet. White sherries—finos and manzanillas— are aged under a layer of yeast known as flor, so that the oxygen doesn't get to them. Brown sherries—olorosos, amontillado, and palo cortados—are aged with oxygen contact, so they darken and take on the flavor of nuts. These wines are all fortified after fermentation so they contain very little sugar. Finally, there are sweet wines made from Pedro Ximénez grapes, which taste of raisins. Wines from these three categories might be blended

Sherry? Don't mind if I do, especially when served like this (*above*). A sherry decanter and glasses on a traditional silver tray in the library at Tatton Hall, in Cheshire, England.

together to create "granny" sherries like Harvey's Bristol Cream, which though much maligned can actually taste very nice.

Finos and manzanillas (just like a fino but from the seaside town of Sanlúcar de Barrameda) are bone dry and only very lightly fortified to 15%. They are great for drinking cold with lots of seafood. The brand leaders Tio Pepe and La Gitana are both excellent, though you can find more interesting as well as more expensive wines from smaller producers such as Bodegas Tradicion or Fernando de Castilla.

Amontillados start their life as finos, but then the flor dies and they age with exposure to oxygen to take on aromas of hazelnuts, almonds, and sometimes butterscotch. They're great with hard cheeses and aged ham. Olorosos are sherries that never grew a flor and so have been aged entirely oxidatively, which gives them dark flavors of molasses and walnuts. They tend to be less elegant than amontillados—the name oloroso means pungent in Spanish. Finally, there's a style known as palo cortado, which is a sort of cross between the two. All three are fortified to about 18% and are normally dry.

Finally, PX sherry is made from super-sweet raisined Pedro Ziménez grapes. It is one of the sweetest wines known to man and can last for years. It's quite spectacular in tiny amounts on its own, but it is usually used as a sweetening agent in sherries such as the spectacular Matusalem Muy Viejo from González Byass. Sherry can be a magical cocktail ingredient: a teaspoon of PX can take an Old Fashioned to a whole new level and a splash of fino will perk up a Bloody Mary.

A bottle of dark or sweet sherry should last a few weeks open, but a fino needs to be drunk within a couple of days. I generally have a bottle of fino in the fridge and something dark out on the side, like Amontillado Napoleon Seco from Hidalgo.

MARSALA

This sadly neglected fortified wine comes from Sicily. It is mostly just used for cooking now, but vergine (unsweetened) marsalas can be excellent if rarely cheap. De Bartoli is the best producer, but don't discount the top vergines from the big boys such as Florio or Pellegrino.

Champagne is a wonderfully versatile cocktail ingredient (*left*). The Twinkle, a mixture of champagne, vodka, and elderflower cordial, invented by bartender Tony Conigliaro from 69 Colebrooke Row in London, has become a modern classic.

MADEIRA

Immortal wine from a Portuguese island off the coast of west Africa, Madeira can last 150 years. I've had wines from the 1860s that still taste a bit young. As part of the production process wines are either left out in the sun or gently heated, which gives a slightly burnt taste. The quality wines are made from single grape varieties: sercial is the driest, followed by verdelho and bual. Finally there is malmsey/malvasia, which is intensely sweet.

SOUTHERN FRANCE

The Roussillon, the bit of France that thinks it's in Spain, is home to some wonderful and very underpriced fortified sweet wines. There are Banyuls and Maury, which are made from red grapes similar to port, and like port can either be bottle-aged or left out in the sun in old casks like Madeira. Rivesaltes is similar, but usually made from white grapes. After 30 years aging, an old Rivesaltes will look much like an old Banyuls.

AUSTRALIA

The Australian wine industry was built on fortified wines, such as Empire ports for the British market. These wines are now rare, but worth seeking out as they can be superb. Look for tawnies, port-style wines from the Barossa Valley or super-sweet muscats from Rutherglen, which, again, are aged a bit like Madeira in hot sheds.

PINEAU DES CHARENTES AND FLOC DE GASCOGNE

Not strictly wines, these are made from grape juice fortified with either cognac (Pineau des Charentes, aged in old cognac barrels) or armagnac (Floc de Gascogne, normally sold young and fresh). They are both intensely sweet and the French drink them as aperitifs. For the rest of us they work better after a meal with cheese.

SPARKLING WINES

CHAMPAGNE

I have drunk a lot of champagne in my life and my hard-won wisdom is this: it's worth not cutting corners when buying champagne. The very cheap stuff is rarely worth drinking. The vineyard land in Champagne is the most sought after in France, which makes the grapes expensive to buy, the production method takes time and then the champagne needs to rest for a year or two minimum. If you want to save money, you'd be much better going for something from Australia, New Zealand or Spain.

Champagne is made in northern France, about as far north as it's possible to ripen grapes properly. The grapes are pinot noir and pinot meunier (both red) and chardonnay (a white grape). There are also small quantities of other grapes grown, but they are rarely seen. The grapes are harvested in the Fall and then made into a still wine. The highly acidic and not terribly delicious wines are blended with wines from previous vintages into a house style, bottled with added wine, yeast, and sugar, then sealed, and left to ferment a second time. The resulting carbon dioxide trapped in the heavy glass bottles is absorbed into the wine. Voila! Bubbles! It's left in this state for a minimum of 15 months. Two processes, riddling and disgorgement, remove yeast cells. The wine is then topped up with some sweetened wine, corked and either sold or ideally left to mature longer.

Champagne's problem is that it's so easy to sell that cheaper ones are produced from inferior wines made from unripe grapes, not matured long enough and the deficiencies covered up with sugar. Champagne needs high-quality grapes and time to soften for those lovely biscuit flavors to develop. Of the big names I'm particularly partial to Pol Roger and Louis Roederer. Vintage wines—wines from a particular year—from both these producers tend to be superb, usually as good as the very expensive wines, such as Krug, Dom Pérignon, etc.

These companies are known as Grand Marques. They make millions of bottles of wine a year and though they own their own vineyards they also buy in grapes from farmers around the region. If you look on the back label of champagne from a big house it will say NM, standing for *négociant manipulant*. You might also find RM on the label, *récoltant manipulant*, which means a grower-maker i.e. they grow all their own grapes. This category includes excellent producers such as Fleury and Edmond Barnaut, which are often cheaper than the big names, though other growers such as Jacques Selosse have attained cult status with prices to match. Finally there's CM, a co-operative, indicating large groups of growers who have clubbed together to make wines. Most supermarket own labels are made by co-ops, and they can be good if not exactly magical.

Champagne can be made from all dark grapes when it's known as Blanc de Noirs, all chardonnay, (Blanc de Blanc) or it can be rosé, which is made either by leaving some of the dark skins in the wine for a short time or simply by adding red pinot noir wine. Most champagne is brut, which means it has less than 12g of sugar per liter, but you also get extra dry, which is sweeter, and demi-sec, which is sweeter still. These sweeter wines are rarely seen. You also get brut nature, which has no added sugar.

It is very easy to develop expensive tastes very quickly, and it really is worth spending a bit more money and drinking less of it or going outside the region if you're having a big party. But one thing to remember with champagne is that though the entry point for good wine is high, very quickly you are in the top echelons. A bottle of vintage Pol Roger or Krug Grand Cuvée will set you back between $100 and $260. Both will be sold ready

to drink and will be guaranteed excellent. Compare that with a bottle of mature first-growth Bordeaux, cult Californian wine or Grand Cru Burgundy, and suddenly champagne looks like a bargain. Champagne is cheap, if you spend enough money.

OTHER SPARKLING WINES

Very good champagne-style sparkling wines are made in Australia and especially Tasmania (Jansz), California (Domaine Carneros, Mumm Napa), New Zealand (Lindauer), and, unusually, England (Gusbourne Estate, Nyetimber). Cava is getting better the whole time and producers such as Gramona are hitting champagne heights. Segura Viudas and Juvé y Campos make good Cava at all price points. And don't forget France has a whole host of sparkling wines, such as Blanquette de Limoux (normally slightly sweet), Crémant de Bourgogne (can do a convincing champagne impersonation) and Saumur from the Loire (reliably delicious).

PROSECCO

Most sparkling wines are made in the image of champagne, but Prosecco used a different process. The secondary fermentation takes place in a tank and then the wines are filtered and bottled under pressure. This method is less labor intensive and unlike champagne, Prosecco can be sold straight away. Not only is this method cheaper, but it also preserves fresh fruit flavors.

Only wines from the Prosecco region not far from Venice can be called Prosecco. The principal grape is called glera (it used to be called Prosecco but the wily Italians changed the name so that the Australians couldn't use the magic word Prosecco

Champagne is combined with apple and elderflower liqueur to create the Textures of Apple and Elderflower, as served at the American Bar of the Savoy Hotel in London (**opposite**).

on their bottles.) Prosecco tends to be sweeter than champagne. Confusingly, wines labeled dry are actually quite sweet; extra dry is drier though still contains between $\frac{1}{4}$– $\frac{1}{2}$ oz (12–17g) of sugar. If you want a proper dry wine look for the word brut on the label. The term frizzante, as opposed to spumante, means that the wine is less fizzy.

Prosecco is a fun, frivolous wine, so don't be afraid to mix it with peach juice to make a Bellini, with Aperol or Campari to make a spritz or, most hedonistic of all, lemon ice cream and vodka, which is called a sgroppino.

TABLE WINES

Your first question should be, what do you want from your wine? Do you want something to drink fairly unthinkingly while watching television, do you want something to enhance your food or do you want something that will be an evening's entertainment in itself? Who will you be drinking it with? Is it your partner on your anniversary or has Steve from accounts just popped over? Here is a very brief and completely personal guide to wine.

SERVING WINES

Old wines, such as vintage port or claret, will need to be decanted, as there will be lots of sediment. I find that the older the wine, the later you should decant. Very old wines can fall apart quickly when exposed to oxygen. Conversely very young wines, especially tannic ones, benefit from air contact, so are worth decanting well in advance. Some more serious whites can benefit from aeration as well. I once drank a bottle of Chateau Musar Blanc, a wine from Lebanon, over the course of three days and every day it showed more complexity.

Reds should not be served too warm (50 to 65° Fahrenheit)—the lighter the red the cooler you can serve it. And whites should not be too cold (45 to 48° Fahrenheit); the better the white, the better it will taste with a bit of warmth. Wine professionals talk about the 20/20 rule: reds should spend 20 minutes in the refrigerator before serving and whites should be taken out 20 minutes before serving. It's good rule of thumb, though does depend on the wine, and how warm your house.

WINES TO KEEP

This section could be headlined "wines you can't afford." These are wines to put in your cellar and forget about for 5, 10, even 20 years. You'll need proper storage facilities.

In the olden days if you were a French or English gentleman this would have meant classed-growth Bordeaux: wines such as Latour or, a little further down the ranking, Léoville Barton. More modern versions of this include cabernets from Napa Valley, California, Coonawarra in Australia, and Bolgheri in Italy, which are made in the image of Bordeaux, though sometimes surpass it in quality.

It would have also have meant Burgundy, grand and premier crus from Côte de Nuits or Côte de Beaune. Outside Burgundy look for pinot noirs from Sonoma in California, Mornington Peninsula in Australia, and Ayr in Germany.

Then there are wines from the Rhône, syrah-based in the north (Hermitage and Côte-Rôtie), and grenache-based (Châteauneuf) in the south. And, of course, there are new-world equivalents, particularly from Australia, which excels in Rhône varieties. Santa Barbara in California makes some mind-bogglingly good syrahs. Other wines to keep include Chianti Classico and the three Bs from Italy—Brunello, Barbaresco, and Barolo—and Rioja and Ribera del Duero from Spain.

For whites, the traditional wines for keeping include the very best Rieslings from Germany, Alsace and Austria and white Burgundy, as well as the best Californian, Australian and New Zealand chardonnay. Finally, there are the great sweet wines, such as Sauternes, Tokaji, and Beerenauslesen, from Germany.

WINES TO DRINK

So you've filled your cellar with classed-growth Bordeaux. What are you going to drink while you wait for it to mature? This is a very concise personal list of what I usually have in the house for everyday drinking:

Reds

I normally have a few wines from the Rhône or something similar in the house. These are wines based on syrah, grenache, mourvèdre, and others. The Languedoc, Spain, and Australia offer similar sort of wines. Also some lighter reds from the Loire or Beaujolais that can take a light chilling on a hot day. Greece and Portugal, for my mind the two most exciting places on earth for wine, both have a wealth of grape varieties not found anywhere else. Finally, I usually have some Rioja.

Whites

My house white is usually a Vinho Verde, something very crisp and fresh from northern Portugal, a lemony Greek wine such as an Assyrtiko, or perhaps a dry German Riesling. I normally have some ordinary Bourgogne Blanc in the house or something similar from Australia, New Zealand or South Africa. Sauvignon Blanc from either the Loire or New Zealand is a real crowd-pleaser, but it is worth spending a bit more money as the bottom end can be a bit industrial. For better value, look for Chenin Blanc from the Loire or South Africa.

A good wine glass such as this should let you admire the color of the wine as well as curving inwards a little at the rim to allow you to appreciate the aroma (*right*).

Rosé

Rosé is such a good all-rounder as it goes with pretty much any food. I love those very pale rosés from Provence, especially those from the town of Bandol, but I'm also partial to gutsier, darker pinks from the Rhône, Italy, and Australia.

BEER

Last year I was in Paris with my wife and we stumbled across a bar that was swarming with super-trendy Parisians. Rather than drinking pastis or wine, they were drinking beer, and not just any beer but British beer, IPA. Of course, being French they were drinking it out of wine glasses and doing far more smoking, flirting, and gesticulating than actual drinking, but still British beer! In Paris! Who could have predicted that ten years ago?

It's not just France though, but Spain, Italy, Japan—the whole world seems to have gone mad for beer, with small brewers popping up all over the place. I even had a superb local beer in Beirut. While non-traditional beer countries embrace grain and hops, the brewing scenes in beer's heartlands—Germany, Belgium, the Czech Republic, and Britain—have been revitalized, with old styles being rediscovered and new ones being created. India Pale Lager, anyone?

Much of this reinvigoration came from the States, where beer enthusiasts in the '70s and '80s, tired of the bland offerings from the big brewers, decided to start making their own. They were, on the whole, inspired by British brewing, so they took almost extinct styles such as IPA (India Pale Ale) or Imperial Porter and added a hefty dose of new-world optimism to make beers with big bold flavors. These in turn inspired brewers around the world, not least in the original home of these beers. Nowadays you get English brewers trying to make American-style IPAs and Americans trying to make English ones.

Before we look at the different beer styles out there, some basics. Beer consists of malted barley, yeast, and hops, though you might also find fruit, honey, herbs, spices, or even seafood in your beer. Yes, really—I had a beer brewed with lobsters that was surprisingly delicious. Hops, a pungent plant related to cannabis, provides that characteristic bitter taste. American IPAs owe their distinctive aroma to American strains of hops. Hops not only taste delicious, but act as a preservative. There are two types of yeast used in brewing. Top-fermenting yeasts are used to make ales, so-called because they float to the top after fermentation, and bottom-fermenting yeasts are used in making lager, a beer that is brewed at a very low temperature. You also have some beers that are fermented with wild yeasts i.e. yeasts that are in the atmosphere, rather than special yeasts developed for beer production. Beer's color comes from malted barley. In the malting process the grain is treated to turn starch into fermentable sugar. This process can be done so that the color of the barley stays light, resulting in pale beers, or it can be heavily toasted, producing the characteristic color and chocolate/coffee flavors of stout.

The world is now a very exciting place for a beer drinker, but it can also be a confusing place. New breweries appear the whole time, while sadly many go out of business, so I have recommended established names. To the proper beer geek this list will seem a bit staid. I've tried to divide beer into categories for your well-stocked bar, but beer styles are hard to categorize. One man's porter will be another's stout, and there's nothing beer geeks love more than a disagreement about style.

STORING AND SERVING BEER

As with wine, temperature is important. A lager should usually be drunk colder than an ale, but, except with the cheapest stuff, don't freeze them to death or you won't be able to taste anything. There's a myth that English beer should be warm. It should be cellar temperature, warm in comparison with pilsner lager, but certainly not the room temperature of a centrally heated house. Most beer will be filtered, but some will contain live yeasts. If you want a perfectly clear pint, then you'll need to pour carefully, though I don't really mind a little yeast in my beer. Nowadays canning technology has improved to the extent that some excellent beers are now sold in cans, so don't turn your nose up at them.

LAGER

After you've been working in the garden or just lazing by the pool, you don't want a big, heavy hoppy IPA or treacly porter— what you want is a nice cold lager. Something like Heineken is perfectly fine, but it's worth going for something like Pilsner Urquell from the Czech Republic, which has a lot more bite to it.

Lager is now the dominant beer style around the world. The word comes from a German word meaning "to store." Lager was originally kept in cold cellars to mature for a few months before selling. Most mass-market lager will not have had this "lagering" process. There are many different styles and colors of lager, but the archetype for the word beer, a crisp, hoppy golden beer, was created in the 19th century in Pilsen, which is now in the Czech Republic, but was then part of the Austro-Hungarian Empire. This town still makes some of the best lagers in the world.

Other styles of lagers include Vienna, a malty amber-colored beer (Brooklyn Brewery in the US make a widely available version), Helles, a pale Bavarian lager, and Dunkel, a dark lager from Germany. Boks are strong malty lagers, usually brewed for the winter months.

WHEAT BEERS

Beers brewed with wheat rather than barley have a characteristic cloudy appearance, but that distinctive banana taste comes not from the wheat but from a special yeast used for fermentation. They are very popular in Germany (Erdinger is the big name) and Belgium (Hoegaarden do a very popular one, flavored with coriander and orange peel).

Serving your beer in the right glass can work wonders for your enjoyment (*below*). Pint glasses are fine for light English bitters, but strong Belgian ales should be served in vessels that look more like wine glasses.

IPA

This style of beer evolved for the long voyage from England to India, which could take up to six months through tropical waters. The journey was hard on beers, but one particular beer, from Hodgson's brewery in Bow, east London, loaded with preserving hops and alcohol, actually improved on the journey. It became the toast of British India, the beer of officers and the upper classes. IPA evolved into Pale Ale, a slightly lower alcohol and more lightly hopped version, which, in the form of Bass from Burton-on-Trent, became the world's first global beer brand.

But back at home, due to the shortages of Word War I, beer became weaker and true IPA died out in its home country, with a few notable exceptions, such as Worthington's White Shield. It was thanks to the Americans that this style has been revived so successfully that even the Germans are making IPAs. You now get all kinds of IPAs: dark IPAs (surely a contradiction in terms) and even fruit IPAs—not a good idea.

Greenwich Brewery in south London make a superb 19th-century-style IPA. Conditioned in a wine bottle (meaning the fizz comes from fermentation in bottle, rather than carbonation), it's one that will improve with age. Goose Island in Chicago shows what can be done with the bold American style.

BITTERS AND ALES

Bitter, descended from IPA, is the classic beer in English pubs. Low in alcohol but not in flavor, it's the ultimate session beer. The bottled stuff tends to be slightly higher in alcohol and never tastes quite as good, so if you're entertaining it's worth buying a small barrel. My favorites are Timothy Taylor's Landlord, with its pronounced seville orange character, and Harvey's Sussex Best, which has a (very enjoyable) sulphurous note.

Nowadays in England the word ale is pretty much synonymous with beer, so Fuller's ESB—Extra Special Bitter—is described by the brewery as "the Champion Ale." But the word ale in English was an old word for beer that predated the introduction of hops in the 16th century. So it used to mean an unhopped beer that might be flavored with herbs or spices. Most ales are now hopped, but the word is often kept for sweeter stronger beers, especially those that are aged (see pages 170–1).

Belgium has a rich tradition of ale brewing, sometimes based on British styles that have died out at home, for example, Scotch Ale. Belgian ales come in all kinds of colors. The most famous, such as Chimay, are made at Trappist monasteries.

PORTER/STOUT

A beer made from malt that has been heavily roasted, hence that distinctive color, porter was originally a London style, a dark beer of around 7% alcohol named after the men who drank it, the street porters who carried goods around the City of London. It provided alcohol and refreshment, but also a significant number of the calories that a working man needed. Porter was replaced in the capital's affections by crisp, refreshing pale ale brewed in Burton-on-Trent. Porter, however, in the form of Guinness stout (the word stout simply means strong) would go on to become the beer of Ireland and one of the bestselling beers on earth. Ordinary Guinness is fine, but if you want to try something similar to what a London porter would have drunk try Guinness Foreign Extra stout; it's sweet and strong and has a distinctive acidic tang. You can also buy versions brewed all over the world, including Nigeria, Jamaica, and Singapore. Very strong beers, known as Baltic or Imperial porters, were originally brewed for Tsarist Russia. Again this classic style is being revived. Porterhouse brewery in Dublins make a fine strong Imperial porter.

BARREL-AGED BEERS

London porter was originally matured in huge oak vats, where it picked up a wine-like tang. It was then blended with younger mild beer and sold in pubs. You can taste this technique in the red ale from Belgium, Rodenbach Grand Cru, which is a blend of oak-aged beer and young beer. In fact, brewer Eugène Rodenbach was inspired to make beer in this style in the late 19th century following a visit to London. It has a wonderful refreshing sour note, like biting into a cherry. Greene King in England makes Olde Suffolk ale, too, which is a blend of aged and young beer, too. There are now lots of breweries around the world experimenting with wood aging. Very strong beers are particularly suited to this technique; after some time in barrel, they taste more like port than beer.

WILD BEERS

The vast majority of beers are made with cultured yeast. This doesn't mean that it goes to the theater, it means that it's a specific strain that has been isolated by the brewery to provide a certain taste and to produce alcohol reliably and cleanly.

Some breweries, particularly in Belgium, but also in Latvia and increasingly in Britain and America, do things the old way. They let natural yeasts in the atmosphere do the fermentation (as many wine producers do). The advantage is that you get lots of different yeasts all doing slightly different things and producing different flavors. One particular yeast is called brettanomyces, which in small quantities produces a savory quality, but too much of it makes beer smell of old dogs. The word "brettanomyces" means British yeast; it's the flavor that made London porter so prized. Wild yeasts are unpredictable, so you run the risk of your beer to turning to vinegar. Some beers, such as Rodenbach, are fermented with cultured yeasts and then aged in barrels rich with brettanomyces.

Lambic beers from Belgium are the best-known examples of purely wild beers. Try Boon Oude Geuze, a bottle-fermented blend of lambics. The most accessible versions are fermented with fruit, usually cherries, the sweetness of which balances out the sourness of the beer. Lindemans makes a good example that has the added benefit of only being 3.5% alcohol.

The beer world is a much more varied place than it was ten years ago (*below*). Here is a classic line-up including beers from England, (Worthington's White Shield), the US (Anchor Steam), and Belgium (Trappistes Rochefort).

NON-ALCOHOLIC ESSENTIALS

It's very easy when stocking your bar to forget that you will also need some items that aren't alcoholic. But remember, man cannot live on beer (or wine or Campari) alone.

FRUIT AND VEGETABLES

- **Citrus fruits** Your best friend behind the bar: make sure you always have piles of lemons, limes, and oranges plus a grapefruit or two. Ideally unwaxed fruit as you will be using the skin.
- **Other fruits** Useful fruits include strawberries, blackberries, raspberries, bananas, peaches, and pineapples. Remember that every drink requiring fruit juice or pulp will taste a thousand times better if you use the fresh stuff. (Except with tomatoes—I don't know anyone who makes their own tomato juice.)
- **Celery** If you're a Bloody Mary enthusiast.
- **Herbs** Mint is the most useful, but basil crops up in the Green Park cocktail (see page 214). The Spanish like to put a sprig of rosemary in a G&T.

STORE-CUPBOARD GOODS

- **Snacks** Nibbles such as potato chips, peanuts, pistachios, pretzel pieces—there's nothing better than a salty snack when drinking.
- **Maraschino cherries** Luxardo is the best brand.
- **Good olives** Not those that taste of mouthwash used in cheap pizzerias. You'll need two sorts: a good-quality pitted one for Martinis, especially those giant ones stuffed with almonds, and then something meatier and unpitted for eating. I'm particularly partial to Kalamata olives and those bright green ones from Puglia.
- **Eggs** The whites are for making fizzes, or use the entire egg in old colonial cocktails like Flips. You can buy pasteurized egg whites in cartons, but they will need more shaking than fresh ones.
- **Coffee** If you make a lot of Espresso Martinis it might be worth getting a Nespresso machine. Or a stovetop moka pot is a good substitute. Don't use instant, or your guests will hate you.
- **Sugar** White granulated and a darker sugar like a muscovado for more flavor.
- **Sugar syrup** You can buy ready-made syrup de gomme, which is fine, but make sure it is made from cane sugar rather than corn syrup. But it is very easy and cheap to make your own, which can be flavored (see page 246–7).
- **Condiments** Salt, Worcestershire sauce, pepper, tabasco, celery salt, cinnamon, and nutmeg.

MIXERS

- **Fizzy water** If you don't have a soda syphon buy water in small bottles so that it is always fizzy. Make sure you have lots of it.
- **Rose's Lime Juice Cordial** Not a juice at all, but a cordial made from lime and sugar. You can't make a Gimlet without it. Also very good mixed with gin and soda water in a long drink.
- **Flavored syrups** The two big ones are grenadine, supposedly flavored with pomegranate, used in making a Singapore Sling, and orgeat syrup, made from almonds and rosewater, for Mai Tais. Low-quality syrups gave cocktails a bad name in the '80s and '90s. Most of the big brands of grenadine have never seen a real pomegranate. Instead, they are made from high-fructose corn syrup and artificially flavored, so check the bottle before buying. There's no point investing in high-quality gin if you're going to add what are essentially slushy syrups.

Many bartenders make their own instead (see pages 246–47 for some recipes), but there are some excellent syrups on the market now. B.G. Reynolds is a bartender from Portland, Oregon

Don't skimp on the non-alcoholic ingredients (*above*). This tray contains ingredients essential to make a Bloody Mary, an Old Fashioned, a Martini, and many others.

who, fed up with the quality of commercial syrups, began making his own. Royal Rose in the US makes very good small-batch syrups from natural ingredients. An English company, Jeffrey's, makes tonic syrups in different flavors. I like them as they give just a hint of sweetness and quinine to my gin rather than the full whack of a tradtional G&T.

- **Tonic water** This is sweetened sparkling water containing quinine. It was originally drunk for its antimalarial properties, with the addition of gin to disguise the taste. Sadly, quality took a nosedive in the '70s and '80s. The leading brands became sweetened with artificial sweeteners or high-fructose corn syrup. Drink books and columns used to be full of tips for how to get hold of decent tonic water. G&T connoisseurs would tell you that you needed to buy it in France or try a particular supermarket-owned label.

  There was clearly a massive gap in the market for naturally flavored tonic, which nobody spotted until Fever Tree came along in 2005. Their superior product is made from cane sugar, natural oils, and, of course, quinine bark. You could actually taste the gin. The gin explosion went hand in hand with the tonic renaissance. Fever Tree now offers lots of flavors and it has plenty of rivals. I can recommend Sicilian lemon tonic from Franklin & Sons. In certain bars they offer you a list of tonics. But despite all this tonic diversity, some people still swear by Schweppes.

- **Ginger beer** A great all-rounder, especially with whisky and rum. Fentimans is delicious, with a big hit of ginger and not too much sugar. Old Jamaica is extremely sweet, so I normally cut it with a little fizzy water and lemon/lime juice.

- **Tomato juice** Just as with orange juice, there are good and bad ones in the supermarkets. For Bloody Marys I am partial to Big Tom spiced tomato juice.

- **Coca-Cola** Full fat please, and always out of a small can or bottle. It must be very cold and very fizzy.

APERITIFS AND COCKTAILS

I've had fun in this section choosing favorite cocktails, but there are also more avant garde recipes from some of the world's most innovative bartenders to try when you've mastered the classics.

MUDDLING IT UP

Cocktails require care. As I pointed out earlier, making cocktails is more like baking than cooking, so everything has to be in the correct quantity or the magic won't happen. But your lemons might be sweeter or sourer than the ones I use, your gin might be stronger, your taste might be different. So keep tasting the whole time. If it doesn't taste right then play with the ratios a bit. Except in a couple of cases, such as Campari, I haven't specified any particular brands.

There's nothing here to frighten the novice: no foams, no layering, or anything that requires a centrifuge. Straight up means that it's served with no ice in the glass. Double-strained means that you use a separate strainer in addition to the one built into the shaker. At the end of the chapter are some simple syrup and bitters recipes, plus a couple more elaborate concoctions if you're feeling adventurous (see pages 246–9). That's it, I think. Let's cocktail!

Care, precision, and practice are required to make the perfect cocktail. Here a bartender is double straining a concoction into a tumbler with ice (*previous pages*).

Clinking ice in frosted shakers tells the story of these five bartenders in Havana, Cuba, competing in the finals of the annual cocktail-mixing contest to determine which of the thousands in Havana is the cocktail champion (*above*).

One thing all Martini lovers agree on is that James Bond is wrong; a Martini should be stirred, as demonstrated here, not shaken—shaking introduces air and ice crystals and ruins the whole thing (*opposite*).

GIN COCKTAILS

MARTINI

There's a lot of macho talk about Martinis. You know the sort of things: show the gin a bottle of vermouth, throw the vermouth in the garbage bin, and then drink the gin. The Martini's ancestor is a cocktail popular in the 1880s, the Martinez, made with sweet Old Tom gin, sweet vermouth, and bitters. As it became drier, the Martinez evolved into the Martini, and it kept getting drier and drier. Ernest Hemingway specified a ratio of 15 parts gin to 1 part vermouth. Bernard DeVoto, however, the poet of the cocktail hour, specified 3.690412 parts gin to 1 part vermouth. You'll need some serious measuring equipment for that.

The Martini is an adaptable beast and can take a lot of tinkering. If you're going to use vodka, use one with as much flavor and body as you can find. You don't want something that tastes of nothing. Unaged armagnac is peppery and spicy and makes a great substitute. You can use fino sherry instead of vermouth, especially with a drop of sugar syrup and a dash of orange bitters. After much playing around, here's my ideal recipe. I like a Martini where you can actually taste the vermouth.

2 fl oz (60ml) gin
¼ fl oz (10ml) dry vermouth

Keep your gin in the freezer and ideally your glasses, too. Fill a decanter with lots of ice, pour in the gin and vermouth, stir vigorously for 30 seconds. Strain into a Martini glass and *serve with a twist of lemon or two almond-stuffed olives if you're hungry.*

BRONX

This is perhaps *the* cocktail of the 1920s. It's a bit like a Martini, but made with orange juice. It was invented in 1906 at the Waldorf Astoria hotel in New York (obviously) by a bartender called Johnnie Solon. The Bronx, however, had to wait until Prohibition before it had its moment. All that orange juice was perfect for disguising the taste of dodgy gin. Which is perhaps why it is rather an obscure cocktail these days, now that we have good gin coming out of our ears. The borough itself, the Bronx, has insalubrious connotations compared with glamorous Manhattan and hip Brooklyn, so that might explain why nobody makes it anymore. Also it has been debased by being made with concentrated orange juice. If you use freshly squeezed or—my own favorite—fresh blood orange juice, then it's a marvelous concoction.

You can add a few drops of Angostura bitters, in which case it is called an Income Tax. (Who comes up with these names?) To turn a Bronx into a Queens, swap the orange juice for pineapple juice, combine the two or add a bit of lemon (depending on the recipe you use). There is still a gap in the market for a Staten Island cocktail.

2 fl oz (50ml) gin
1 fl oz (25ml) Italian vermouth
½ fl oz (15ml) French vermouth
1 fl oz (30ml) freshly squeezed orange juice
dash of orange bitters

Shake all the ingredients and strain into a cold Martini glass. *Garnish with an orange twist.*

JIM MEEHAN *from PDT, New York City*

Jim Meehan is the man behind New York bar PDT (Please Don't Tell), which opened in 2013 and pioneered the trend for Speakeasy-style bars that are now such a fixture of the urban landscape. PDT is located in a nondescript hot dog shop in the East Village, and you enter via a telephone booth. Meehan is also a journalist and author of two classic books: *The PDT Cocktail Book* (2011) and *Meehan's Bartender Manual* (2017). This is one of the recipes from the latter. There are quite a few different cocktails going under the name Rosy Cheeks, normally based on gin, but this is surely the most decadent incarnation. The sloe gin gives it a beautiful reddish hue, and the Crème de Cacao brings out chocolate notes in the Irish whiskey. It's sure to bring the color to your cheeks.

Rosy Cheeks

¾ fl oz (20ml) Redbreast 12-year-old
    Single Pot Still Irish Whiskey
½ fl oz (15ml) Plymouth Sloe Gin
½ fl oz (15ml) Tempus Fugit
    Crème de Cacao (Dark)
½ fl oz (15ml) lemon juice
2 fl oz (60ml) Perrier-Jouët Champagne

Stir with ice in a shaker, then fine strain into a chilled wine glass filled with ice. Top with the champagne. *Garnish with a lemon wheel.*

ERIC LORENZ *from the Savoy, London*

The American Bar at the Savoy in London is definitely a contender for the most famous bar in the world. Its legendary head bartender was Harry Craddock, author of *The Savoy Cocktail Book*, who worked there from 1920 to 1938. So Eric Lorenz, originally from Slovakia, was stepping into some enormous shoes when he took over in 2010. He said, "Once you become head bartender at the Savoy, you will always be head bartender at the Savoy." This is his signature cocktail, named after the nearby park and, of course, all that green basil in the drink. Make sure you use the freshest basil you can get your hands on. The Green Park harks back to the 19th century by using sweet Old Tom gin rather than the more normal London Dry Gin.

Green Park

1½ fl oz (45ml) Jensen's Old Tom gin
1 fl oz (30ml) lemon juice
½ fl oz (15ml) sugar syrup (2:1 concentration)
3 drops Bitter Truth celery bitters
dash of egg white
6–8 fresh basil leaves

Blend all the ingredients with a hand blender and then shake with ice. Double strain into a coupette or Martini glass.

BRAMBLE

Unusual in this book, a truly British cocktail and one that has an undisputed inventor. Dick Bradsell, who died in 2016, was a legend of the British bar scene. He is best known for his stint at the Atlantic Bar, Piccadilly Circus, which became *the* celebrity hangout of the '90s and early '00s. The Bramble dates back further, to the '80s, when Bradsell was working in a Soho bar called Fred's Club. It was inspired by the British pastime of brambling in late summer, when the blackberry bushes that grow in hedgerows and wasteland come into fruit.

50ml (2 fl oz) dry gin
25ml (1 fl oz) lemon juice
10ml (¼ fl oz) sugar syrup
10ml (¼ fl oz) Crème de Mûre (see page 247 for a recipe to make your own)

Shake the gin, lemon juice, and sugar syrup with ice in a shaker, strain into a tumbler filled with crushed ice. Drizzle Crème de Mûre on the top and *garnish with a bramble that you have ideally foraged yourself.*

FRENCH 75

Named after a French artillery gun, the 75mm, this was invented by Harry MacElhone at Harry's Bar in Paris just after World War I. It's a rather odd mixture of gin and champagne. We forget that people didn't used to be so precious about their wine. It was common to add sugar to champagne, or even do as Queen Victoria did and add whisky. There's little point using your best Krug for this; anything with a bit of body stands up to all those additions. Cava would also work well, though Prosecco is too sweet. I like a high lemon quotient.

1¼ fl oz (35ml) gin
½ fl oz (15ml) fresh lemon juice
1 tsp sugar syrup
3½ fl oz (100ml) champagne
dash of orange bitters

Shake the first three ingredients with ice and strain into a champagne flute. Top up with champagne or Cava (I won't tell), add a dash of bitters and *serve with an orange twist.*

GIN & IT

When I think of the Gin & It, I always think of "It Girls," upper-class English party girls who appear in gossip columns and scandalize polite society with brazen antics in Mayfair nightclubs. But "It" stands for Italian. A Gin & It is a mix of Italian vermouth and gin, usually in equal measures, but you can go heavy on the gin. It's great for showing off fancy boutique vermouth, though Martini Rosso also works.

1¼ fl oz (35ml) gin
1¼ fl oz (35ml) red vermouth
dash of orange bitters

Fill a tumbler with lots of ice, add the gin and the vermouth, stir vigorously, add a dash of bitters, and *garnish with a twist of orange.*

WHISKY AND BRANDY COCKTAILS

OLD FASHIONED

As befits its name, the Old Fashioned dates back to the early 19th century. In fact, some think that it is the first cocktail. It's a very simple beast, essentially just sweetened whiskey, but it's one that requires attention to make it properly. You want to avoid grittiness from the undissolved sugar. Some people use sugar syrup, but then you miss the fun of stirring the sugar so that it dissolves. It's a drink that accentuates the quality of the spirit, so make sure you use a really good whiskey. I recommend Blanton's Small Batch bourbon, but any good American whiskey would work. If you're using rye you might want to up the sugar.

I had the best Old Fashioned I'd ever had at a bar in London, made by a French bartender. His twist was to add dash or two of maraschino liqueur and some PX sherry to sweeten it. Both gave it a nutty complexity that chimed beautifully with the bourbon. If you do this, use a little less sugar.

3 fl oz (80ml) bourbon
1 tsp sugar
2 dashes of Angostura bitters
splash of water

Put the sugar at the bottom of a tumbler, add a couple of good dashes of bitters and a splash of warm water. Using your muddler or a spoon, grind the sugar. Add half the bourbon and stir vigorously (you want all the sugar to dissolve). Add lots of ice and the rest of the bourbon, stir some more and *serve with a maraschino cherry and an orange slice.*

MANHATTAN

As the Martini is to gin so the Manhattan is to whiskey: spirit flavored with vermouth. Americans were drinking whiskey before gin, so you could argue that the Martini is just a gin Manhattan. Like the Martini, the Manhattan has gradually become drier since its invention in late 19th-century New York. Early recipes call for equal parts vermouth to whiskey, as well as sugar syrup. A rye or a drier, spicier bourbon works really well here, as it gives the sweet vermouth something to play against. A very sweet sippin' sort of bourbon wouldn't work quite as well. The next question is whether to shake or stir. I am firmly in the stirring camp but, unlike in a Martini, I think a little dilution isn't such a bad thing here so don't use cold whiskey or vermouth.

You can make your Manhattan "perfect" by using half French and half Italian vermouth. Or dry by using just French. To make a smoky Manhattan try rinsing the glass with a drop or two of Islay whisky first. Or you can make it with Scotch whisky, in which case it becomes a Rob Roy; named after a Broadway musical based on Walter Scott's 1817 novel that was all the rage in 1890s New York when the cocktail was invented.

2 fl oz (50ml) spicy bourbon or rye
1 fl oz (25ml) Italian vermouth
dash of Angostura bitters

Stir with lots of ice in your shaker, strain into a cold martini glass and *garnish with a twist of orange zest.*

From left to right: Brandy Sour (see overleaf), Old Fashioned, Manhattan, Mint Julep (see overleaf).

BRANDY SOUR

This may look like a simple drink, but it's one that requires precision. You want to get the ratio of booze, sour, and sugar exactly right. It's one you should experiment with a bit to suit your taste. For the Brandy Sour you don't want to use your finest XO, but also you don't want to use something rough that you dig out for setting fire to the Christmas pudding. For me, this is where Brandy de Jerez really comes into its own. I find it a bit too sweet, in comparison with cognac, but this very sweetness makes it the ideal foil to the sourness of lemon juice.

There are so many different variations on the sour principle. You can use pisco (a sort of unaged Peruvian/Chilean brandy), gin, rum, amaretto, bourbon, Metaxa (a Greek brandy flavored with muscat grape juice), or anything really. Just adjust the sugar and sour ratio depending on how sweet your spirit is. Add triple sec or Grand Marnier to a Brandy Sour and you have a Sidecar (five parts brandy, two parts lemon juice, two parts triple sec). You can add a dash of bitters, Angostura or otherwise, or an egg white for texture. You could use PX sherry to sweeten—that would work especially well if you were using Brandy de Jerez. You could even serve it over ice in a tumbler. Here's a basic recipe that you can play around with.

2 fl oz (50ml) brandy
½ fl oz (15ml) lemon juice
¼ fl oz (10ml) sugar syrup

Shake all the ingredients together hard and quickly with lots of ice (you don't want too much dilution). Strain into a coup and *garnish with a maraschino cherry.*

MINT JULEP

The classic drink of the American south, a simple concoction of fresh mint, ice, and whiskey. It's worth using the best-quality bourbon you can find for it. Among cocktail aficionados there's some debate about how much you should smash the mint. Too much and it turns to a pulp, too little and you won't get enough mint flavor. I've taken a leaf (pun intended) out of Kingsley Amis's book: he recommends crushing some mint in advance in a sugar syrup and leaving it for an hour or two to infuse, and then using fresh mint to garnish. My wife, born in Hawaii but with a heart in the Old South, goes one stage further and adds mint when making her sugar syrup (see page 246). You'll also need lots of crushed ice.

My wife then goes on to add some sparkling water and lemon juice to hers, which takes it into Mojito territory. Heretical apparently, but also lovely if you find neat bourbon a bit much on a summer's day. In the past the Julep functioned a bit like a punch, and it was common to add lots of fruit. Henry Pinckney, the White House steward from 1901 to 1909, would make his presidential juleps with a mixture of rye and brandy and then add fruit such as bananas, pineapple, and cherries. You might not want to go this far, but a half of strawberry does look mighty fine. If you've got them use special Julep cups, if not highball glasses.

60ml (2 fl oz) bourbon
20ml (¾ fl oz) mint sugar syrup
5 or so of the juiciest mint leaves you can find

Fill a glass with crushed ice, pour over the bourbon and the syrup, and stir thoroughly. *Garnish with the fresh mint leaves and a strawberry if you fancy it.*

JAKE BLANCH *from Open/Closed, Umeå, Sweden*

Jake Blanch began his career working at his parents' hotel in Brighton. His stepfather Chris Edwards taught him about cocktails, so when he moved to London it seemed obvious to pursue a career in the drinks business. He has worked at some of London's best bars, including Hawksmoor, LAB, Casita, and Kanaloa, but he is best known for working at Mark's Bar in Hix Restaurant in Soho. He is now mixing at a tiny, quirky cocktail bar called Open/Closed, which operates from a deli in the small Swedish city of Umeå.

At Open/Closed they are very into foraging for natural ingredients: the menus have different themes and change every two weeks. More than a Teeling is, however, a little more conventional. It's not dissimilar to a Manhattan, being based on whiskey and vermouth, but the flavors are more delicate as Jake uses a light Irish grain whiskey and a subtly flavored German vermouth, Belsazar Rosé.

More than a Teeling

2 fl oz (50ml) Teelings single grain Irish whiskey
1 fl oz (25ml) Balsazar Rosé vermouth
1 tsp Green Chartreuse
1 tsp sugar syrup
2 dashes of Peychaud's bitters

Stir all the ingredients with ice in your shaker, strain into a Nick & Nora glass with *a grapefruit coin for a garnish.*

ANDY FERREIRA *from Cask, Cork*

This cocktail is inspired by the rugged landscape of Ireland. Cork native Andy Ferreira makes it with foraged ingredients, which thankfully you can also buy online or from health food shops. Dillisk and wakame are kinds of seaweed. They are combined with a peated whiskey, peat being the traditional fuel of this part of Ireland. These native ingredients are then given a Mediterranean twist with the addition of Cocchi Americano, a white aromatized wine made with quinine and grapefruit bitters.

Ferreira spent 12 years traveling and working in bars around the world with stints in San Francisco and New York. Returning to Cork, he spent nine years working in the award-winning Long Island bar before opening his own bar, Cask. He has represented Ireland at the prestigious Cocktail World Cup in New Zealand.

Man of Aran

1½ fl oz (40ml) Connemara peated whiskey
¾ fl oz (20ml) Cocchi Americano
¼ fl oz (7.5ml) smoked wakame sugar syrup
    (see page 246)
grapefruit peel
dillisk

Add all the ingredients except the grapefruit peel and the dillisk to a mixing glass, stir with ice and decant into a Nick and Nora glass or a coupe. Express grapefruit oil over the top (see page 250), then discard the peel. *Garnish with a small piece of dillisk, either sitting across the rim of the glass or pegged to the side.*

FRASER HAMILTON *from Sweet Liberty, Miami*

The Flip is one of the great old-school cocktails. Originally made with sherry, it was very popular in the early 19th century. This one is beefed up with Scotch whisky and a liqueur made from rum and raisins.

Fraser Hamilton is a career bartender who has worked all over the world: Glasgow, Edinburgh, New York, Boston, and Martha's Vineyard. He currently manages Sweet Liberty on Miami Beach, which, according to Fraser, prides itself on "taking basic or recognizable drinks and adding our own interesting touches that you might not think to do in your home bar. We don't want to reinvent the wheel, we just want to make you smile and give you an experience you'll remember and talk about."

Whisky Flip

1 fl oz (30ml) Monkey Shoulder whisky
1 fl oz (30ml) Pedro Ximenez sherry
1 fl oz (30ml) Rum Raisin liqueur (recipe below)
1 whole egg, whipped
2 dashes of Dr Adam Elmegirab's
    Aphrodite Bitters
1 tsp toasted coconut

Combine all the ingredients apart from the coconut and whip in a shaker, then add ice and shake vigorously. Pour into a chilled coupe glass and *garnish with a spoonful of toasted coconut.*

* Rum Raisin liqueur is Wray & Nephew overproof rum infused with raisins and then combined with turbinado sugar syrup.

BROOKLYN

A rather forgotten cocktail now, named after a borough of New York, just like the Manhattan, the Queens and the Bronx. The secret ingredient is Amer Picon, a bitter French drink made with gentian, quinine, and, most importantly, oranges. In fact it tastes a bit like marmalade that has been left on the boil too long—in a good way! It's easy to find in Europe, available in Britain though rather expensive, and impossible to find in the US. So sadly this most New York of cocktails is difficult to make in New York. Bartenders in the States stock up when they are in France and smuggle bottles back into the US, which gives it an illicit Prohibition feel. The interplay between the cherry liqueur and the orangey Picon is quite something. It tastes like a more complex, bitter version of the Manhattan.

If you can't find Amer Picon, there are recipes available to make your own. Or you could use another amari (bitter drink.) A mixture of Averna Amaro, Aperol, and a splash of orange bitters gives the necessary bittersweet orange component. It's one that's worth having fun experimenting with. A Brooklyn is normally served straight up, but there's no reason you couldn't serve it on the rocks like a Boulevardier (see page 236).

1½ fl oz (45ml) bourbon or rye
1½ fl oz (45ml) dry vermouth
¼ fl oz (10ml) Luxardo Maraschino
¼ fl oz (10ml) Picon Amer

Stir with ice and strain into a chilled coupe glass. *Garnish with a cherry.*

SAZERAC

The Sazerac was originally made just with brandy, but when the vineyards of Europe were destroyed by phylloxera (the vine-eating louse that came originally from America in the late 19th century), bourbon was used instead. The Sazerac is *the* New Orleans Cocktail. It was invented in 1838 by Antoine Peychaud, a Louisiana apothecary and inventor of the eponymous bitters. The Sazerac was named after a now defunct make of cognac. Just to confuse matters, Sazerac is now a highly regarded make of rye whiskey, which took its name from the famous cocktail. The maker also owns Buffalo Trace bourbon, Southern Comfort, and Peychaud's bitters, so it has the Cajun cocktail game sewn up.

A Sazerac is not dissimilar to an Old Fashioned. Absinthe can be hard to get hold of, so instead you could use Pernod or Herbsaint, a New Orleans aniseed liqueur, which it won't surprise you to learn is also owned by Sazerac. Almost nobody will know the difference. Some recipes use just bourbon or rye, or you could make a proper old-school one by using just brandy. But whatever you do, you must use Peychaud's or it isn't a Sazerac.

dash of absinthe or absinthe substitute
1 fl oz (30ml) brandy
1 fl oz (30ml) bourbon
1 tsp sugar
dash of Peychaud's bitters

Coat a tumbler with the absinthe. Then, in a shaker, stir together the brandy, bourbon, bitters, and sugar until the sugar has dissolved. Add ice and stir vigorously for about 30 seconds. Strain into an absinthe-coated glass and *serve with a twist of lemon.*

CHARLIE LAMONT *from DaiLo, Toronto*

DaiLo is a Chinese restaurant with French influences, where Charlie Lamont was bar manager for more than two years. He began his career in Glasgow at Blue Dog, then moved to Canada, where he has worked in some of Toronto's top bars, including BarChef and the Miller Tavern.

This cocktail combines some seriously big flavors. Lot 40 is a Canadian whiskey originally launched in the '90s; it gained a cult following but was withdrawn due to lack of sales. It was ahead of its time. Pernod-Ricard relaunched it in 2012, and it is now the go-to Canadian rye for bartenders. Lamont describes it as "the best." Its resinous note is accentuated by the pine syrup.

Shoucheng Moon

2 fl oz (50ml) Lot 40 Canadian Rye
1 tsp pine syrup*
1 tsp Fernet Branca
1 tsp Yellow Chartreuse
3 dashes of Angostura bitters

Stir all the ingredients over ice, strain into chilled coupe glass, and *garnish with a lemon twist.*

* You can buy pine syrup from chemist shops or you can make your own by steeping pine needles in a sugar syrup.

SOTHER TEAGUE *from Amor y Amargo, New York*

Sother Teague is an author, culinary school graduate, bartender, and all-round New York personality. He is the founder of Amor y Amargo, a bar in the East Village, and presents a show called Speakeasy on Brooklyn's Heritage Radio Network. Here is the Pumpernickel in his own words: "My dear friend and colleague Ari would often pour us shots of Rittenhouse and 14 dashes of Angostura bitters. Spicy and gripping! He called it Pumpernickel because it was dark and rye. I've stretched the drink out and included elements of spice from Abano, which smells and tastes of white pepper. As well as the bitterness and body of Punt e Mes, which gracefully ties the line between vermouth and amaro to create a black Manhattan of sorts. Either way, it remains dark and spicy. Now pass me some lox and a schmear, Ari."

Pumpernickel

1½ fl oz (45ml) 100 Proof Rye (I use Rittenhouse)
¾ fl oz (20ml) Luxardo Amaro Abano
¾ fl oz (20ml) Punt e Mes
7 dashes of Angostura bitters
lemon peel

Stir all the ingredients with plenty of ice to chill and dilute. Strain into a chilled rocks glass without ice. (This is referred to as a "down" drink, when a cocktail is served chilled, but not on ice or in a stemmed glass.) Express the oil from a lemon twist over the drink and discard the twist (see page 250).

TROPICAL AND COLONIAL COCKTAILS

MOJITO

Mojitos were the bane of my life in the 1990s. Not that I ever ordered one. It was that whenever I just wanted a pint, there would be someone in front of me ordering nine Mojitos. Thankfully the craze has passed, to be superseded by much easier to make cocktails, such as the Negroni.

The Mojito, or something like it, goes back a long way. It's not dissimilar to grog, the mixture of lime juice, rum, and water that was served to British sailors. Every Caribbean island has their take on this formula. In fact, it's essentially grog mixed with a Mint Julep. It might be a pain to make lots of in a crowded bar, but at home when the pressure's off it's actually very therapeutic crushing the mint and muddling the sugar. The flavor of the rum comes through strongly, so it is worth using something with a bit of flavor, such as Havana Club three-year-old or Mount Gay Eclipse. Just make sure you muddle the sugar thoroughly, as you don't want a gritty drink. You could replace it with syrup or even mint syrup (see page 246.)

approximately 15 fresh mint leaves
2 fl oz (60ml) rum
¾ fl oz (20ml) lime juice
2 tsp fine white sugar
fizzy water

In a highball glass muddle most of the mint, add the rum, sugar, and lime juice, and stir until the sugar has dissolved. Fill the glass with crushed ice, stir thoroughly, and then top up with fizzy water. *Garnish with a sprig of fresh mint.*

SINGAPORE SLING

To add grenadine or not to add grenadine, that is the question. The version of the Singapore Sling that they serve at Raffles Hotel in Singapore is bright red with the stuff and this is where the drink was invented, so you would think that they would serve the definitive version. They even put the recipe proudly on the menu. But according to some booze historians (yes, they do exist) the Raffles version, made with grenadine and pineapple, is a 1970s imposter created for the tourist market, who expected cocktails to look like Mai Tais.

Raffles Hotel credit the drink to a bartender working in the hotel around 1915 called Ngiam Tong Boon. Drinks known as Gin Sling or Straits Sling were common at this time, so this is a version of an older drink. Neither *The Savoy Cocktail Book* (1930) nor David Embury's *The Fine Art of Mixing Drinks* (1948) mention grenadine or pineapple juice. What most recipes do agree on is that a Sling should contain gin, Benedictine, and cherry brandy. This recipe is based on David's.

2 fl oz (50ml) gin
1¼ fl oz (35ml) cherry brandy
½ fl oz (15ml) Benedictine
1 fl oz (30ml) lime juice
1 tsp sugar syrup
dash of Angostura bitters
fizzy water

Shake the first six ingredients with ice and then strain into a tall ice-filled glass and top up with fizzy water. *Serve with a slice of lemon.*

DAIQUIRI

The invention of Cuba's national drink is usually attributed to an American called Jennings Cox, a mining engineer based in the south of the island near Santiago de Cuba. It was the early 20th century and one day he was entertaining some friends when he ran out of gin, the drink Americans usually drank. Rather than let his party break up early, he mixed lime juice, sugar, ice, and water with the local rum, Bacardi, a light, smooth style of spirit that proved ideal for cocktails. With winning modesty Cox named his concoction not after himself, but after the nearby beach, Daiquiri.

It was in Havana, however, that the drink became something unique. The bartender at El Floridita, Constantino Ribalaigua, shook the ingredients with ice and then strained the mixture into a cold glass to create something a little more sophisticated. Emilio Gonzalez at the Plaza Hotel in Cuba came up with the idea of using a blender, a new invention in the 1930s, to crush up ice and fruit to create the frozen Daiquiri.

Nowadays the standard Daiquiri is frozen; if you want an old-school version you have to ask for a Daiquiri Naturale (as per this recipe). The beauty of the Daiquiri is its adaptability: you can use different fruit and rum, you can adjust the sweetness, and it can be frozen or merely cold. Hemingway had a special one without sugar because he was diabetic—it was also a lot stronger. You can make a Daiquiri Mulata with dark rum and coffee liqueur.

2 fl oz (50ml) white rum
½ fl oz (15ml) lime juice
¼ fl oz (10ml) sugar syrup

Shake with ice, pour into a cold glass, and *garnish with a wedge of lime.*

ZOMBIE

The ultimate Tiki cocktail, so if you've filled your lounge with bamboo and invested in a copy of *The Exotic Moods of Les Baxter* you are going to end up making a lot of these. You might even have to invest in some proper Tiki glasses, which look like carved tropical statuettes. The Zombie was invented by Don the Beachcomber (see page 54) in the 1930s. This is a real kitchen sink of a drink. It's got a little bit of everything, including up to four different types of rum: white, overproof, navy, and aged rum.

This seems a little excessive. The most important rum is the aged rum; you want one with a good coconutty flavor from oak aging. You can get by with just the aged and a white rum, though a little spiced rum would be fun, and if you're feeling really frisky then don't omit the overproof rum. And make sure that the grenadine and pineapple juice are of top quality. There's no point mucking about with all those rums if your non-alcoholic ingredients are going to let you down.

1 fl oz (30ml) apricot brandy
1 fl oz (30ml) white rum
1 fl oz (30ml) aged rum
1 fl oz (30ml) lime juice
dash of Angostura bitters
fresh pineapple juice (or try orange or grapefruit)
overproof rum (optional)
1 tbsp grenadine

Shake the first five ingredients with ice, strain into a highball glass filled with ice. Top up with pineapple juice, stir, and then float the overproof rum on the top and drizzle with grenadine so that it sinks into the drink, making a lovely pretty red haze. *Garnish with a wedge of pineapple.* Warning: there is a lot of booze in here.

EOIN KENNY *from the Ham Yard Hotel, London*

This cocktail gets its lurid color from beetroot and requires you to make an infused mezcal. It is inspired by the Mexican Day of the Dead, Día de los Muertos, which takes place around 31 October every year. It's a time when Mexicans honor their dead with colorfully morbid displays.

You might be surprised, therefore, that this cocktails's creator is actually from Australia.

Eoin Kenny cut his teeth at Michelin-starred restaurant Atelier de Joël Robuchon in London, where he invented the Salt and Vinegar Martini, a combination of potato vodka, quince vinegar, liqueurs, and elderflower cordial. He's now Group Mixologist at Firmdale Hotels, a group that includes some of New York and London's most stylish hotels, including the recently opened Ham Yard Hotel in Soho.

Día de los Muertos

2 fl oz (50ml) beetroot Montelobos
    Joven Mezcal*
½ fl oz (15ml) Cynar
¼ fl oz (10ml) Pimento Dram
1 fl oz (30ml) fresh lime juice
¾ fl oz (20ml) agave nectar
dehydrated beetroot

Combine all the ingredients apart from the dehydrated beetroot in a cocktail shaker, shake hard with ice and double strain into a chilled coupette. *Garnish with a dehydrated beetroot chip.*

* Peel 2 fresh beetroot, chop, and combine with 1½ pints (700ml) mezcal. Seal in a vacuum bag and place in a sous-vide at 160° Fahrenheit for 1 hour. Remove and chill. Strain off the mezcal and bottle.

RAMON "EL TIGRE" RAMOS
from Los Barcos in Guadalajara, Mexico

El Tigre spent five years working in bars in London, including a stint at Soho's legendary and much-lamented LAB. While in England he put himself through gastronomy school so he could learn about the science behind food and drink. He has now returned home to Mexico to run his family's restaurant, Los Barcos.

This is his signature cocktail and it makes use of achiote, a paste made from the annatto seed, something used all over Latin America and in Red Leicester cheese. It gives a mild peppery flavor and a vivid color.

Achiote Margarita

2 fl oz (50ml) Altos Blanco tequila
1 fl oz (25ml) fresh lime juice
1 fl oz (25ml) achiote syrup*
¼ fl oz (10ml) agave syrup

Add all the ingredients to a cocktail shaker with lots of ice and shake vigorously for at least 10 seconds, then double strain into a chilled coupette glass and *garnish with a lime wheel.*

* Achiote syrup:
2 pints (1 liter) freshly squeezed orange juice
8 oz (250g) achiote paste
1 cinnamon stick
1 star anise
7 fl oz (200ml) agave syrup

Add the orange juice to a saucepan, whisk in the achiote paste until it dissolves and then add the cinnamon, star anise, and agave syrup. Simmer for 20–25 minutes, but don't let it boil. Take off the heat, strain, and bottle when cooled. It will keep for a month in the refrigerator.

MARGARITA

A drink that will be familiar as the ultimate vacation drink. It's another classic variation on the sweet/sour/booze of the rum punch, but with an added element—salt—that cleverly makes you thirsty while you are drinking. Whoever came up with this one was a genius. There's a reference to a drink in the 1937 *Café Royal Cocktail Book* published in London that is identical, but called the Picador. Nobody is quite sure when it assumed its present name. There are competing stories from different bartenders in Mexico who all claim to have invented the Margarita.

This one couldn't be simpler, but it has to be made from fresh ingredients rather than Margarita mix. You could serve it with crushed ice to make a boozy slushie. Some recipes call for agave syrup rather than triple sec. You can turn your Margarita into a Paloma by adding grapefruit juice (ideally pink as it's sweeter—add some sugar syrup if you don't have pink), fizzy water, and ice. It makes a great long drink for a summer's day. You could use mezcal instead of tequila if you want a stronger drink. A drop of Angostura doesn't go astray.

2 wedges of lime
2 fl oz (50ml) tequila blanco
1 fl oz (25ml) triple sec
1 fl oz (25ml) lime juice
sea salt

Rub a piece of lime around the rim of a margarita class, coupe, or tumbler, and then place the glass rim-side down in some flaky sea salt. Don't use granulated salt. Shake the tequila, triple sec, and lime juice with ice. Strain into your salty glass and *serve with a wedge of lime.*

SHERRY COBBLER

Older even than the Old Fashioned is the Sherry Cobbler. It dates back to before the word cocktail was coined. A Sherry Cobbler is one of the easiest drinks to make as it is simply sherry combined with sugar and served with crushed ice and fruit. Martin Chuzzlewit in the eponymous novel refers to it as a "wonderful invention." Charles Dickens was a great fan of sherry-based drinks. On his gruelling 1867 tour of America, he seemed to take most of his nutrition from sherry flips: a mixture of sherry, eggs, sugar, and nutmeg.

Falstaff calls for a sort of sherry cocktail in *The Merry Wives of Windsor*: "Go fetch me a quart of sack [sherry]; put a toast in't." The Elizabethans drank much of their sherry laced with sugar, spices, and, er, toast. It was a good way of disguising the poor quality of the wine. The Cobbler unites a traditional English way of serving sherry with something that the Americans had lots of: ice.

For this recipe I recommend using a reasonable quality amontillado—you want that nutty taste to come through, though don't use anything too pricey. You could also use an oloroso or a sweetened sherry, in which case cut back on the sugar. Marsala or white port would work well, too. There are all kinds of other Cobblers: champagne, claret, and even sauternes. Garnish with whatever you have on hand. It's essentially a proto-Pimms.

5 fl oz (150ml) brown sherry
1 tsp sugar
dash of orange bitters

Mix the sherry and the sugar, stir until the sugar has dissolved, fill up with crushed ice, add a dash of bitters and stir. *Garnish with a slice of lemon and orange and a sprig of mint.*

ITALIAN APERITIFS

NEGRONI

Here's Tony Bourdain, author, cook, and TV presenter, on the pleasures of the Negroni: "I'm not a gin drinker. I don't like sweet vermouth, I don't like Campari, but together they form a sinister yet lovely and inspired hell broth. Like a marriage, it's a true everlasting love. This is not a cheap date, this is not a one-night stand." Wise words.

The Negroni is usually attributed to Count Camillo Negroni, who, in the 1920s, wanted his Americano made a little stronger in a Florence café. Like a properly fitted suit, a well-made Negroni should grab you by the shoulders, make you stand up straight, and give you a general feeling of importance. Nothing hits the spot quite like it, but be warned, they are powerful and dangerously drinkable. Luckily, unlike most cocktails, with the Negroni there is no rush; they have a very wide timescale of deliciousness, being good strong but also excellent diluted as the ice melts. The best thing after a Negroni is another Negroni, but then you must move on to food or trouble will ensue.

You can have a lot of fun playing around with the formula. It can be served on ice or straight up. Try using half tawny port with the vermouth for added depth. I call this a Christmas Negroni. Swap the gin for whiskey and you have a Boulevardier.

1¼ fl oz (35ml) gin
1¼ fl oz (35ml) red vermouth
1¼ fl oz (35ml) Campari

Stir with lots of ice in a tumbler and *serve with twist of orange.*

AMERICANO

The Americano is James Bond's second favorite cocktail. In the short story "A View to a Kill," Ian Fleming wrote: "One cannot drink seriously in French cafés. Out of doors on a pavement in the sun is no place for vodka or whisky or gin… Bond always had the same thing—an Americano." Bond knew his drinks, even if he did make his Martinis with vodka; you don't want to be drinking nearly neat spirits in the baking heat, especially if you're meant to be ready for action, romantic or violent.

The Americano was a popular drink in the cafés of northern Italy, where it was originally known as a Milano-Torino after its two principal ingredients, Campari from Milan and Martini Rosso from Turin. The name comes from its popularity with American tourists. Now overshadowed by its younger brother the Negroni, the Americano really is the perfect boulevardier drink (much better than a Boulevardier) being full of flavor, but refreshing.

1¼ fl oz (35ml) Campari (or Aperol for a
  milder drink)
1¼ fl oz (35ml) red vermouth (or amber or rosé
  if you are using Aperol)
soda water

Fill your highball glass with ice, add the Campari and vermouth, stir, top with soda water, stir again. *Garnish with a slice of orange.* Leave the stirrer in as the Campari and vermouth will sink. Leave soda on the side so the drink can be diluted if it gets too syrupy.

From left to right: Bellini (see overleaf), Negroni, Aperol Spritz (see overleaf), Americano.

BELLINI

The great drink of Venice, or rather the other great drink of Venice alongside the Aperol spritz (see right). It was invented by Giuseppe Cipriani at Harry's Bar in the 1930s and named after the Venetian painter Giovanni Bellini. To this day the tourists line up at Harry's Bar to be charged through the nose for a cocktail, just as at Raffles in Singapore or El Floridita in Havana. Ideally, you want to use the finest-quality, in-season white Italian peaches, but how are you going to find those in December? You can buy decent quality peach nectar these days, which, while not quite as nice as the real thing, will taste better than a rock-hard, flavorless out-of-season peach. If you do find decent peaches, halve, remove the stone and the skin, and then pulp in a blender.

You really want to use Prosecco in this, firstly because the peaches will overwhelm most champagnes, but also because Prosecco has a sweet, peachy character that's perfect for this drink. You could use freshly squeezed orange juice and you have a Mimosa (or Bucks Fizz as it's known in Britain). Normally this is made with champagne, but I think Prosecco actually works better. You could use grapefruit juice and balance it with a little sugar syrup or indeed Aperol, which brings you to something a bit like Venice's other great drink.

---

1 fl oz (30ml) peach pulp or nectar
1 tsp sugar syrup
6 fl oz (175ml) Prosecco

Make sure all the ingredients are very cold. Add the peach pulp and sugar syrup to a champagne flute, top up with Prosecco, stir, and serve.

APEROL SPRITZ

Venice's other great cocktail (alongside the Bellini). Ten years ago nobody outside of Italy had heard of an Aperol Spritz, and now it seems that every pub on the planet offers them. Most, I am sad to say, do it really badly by putting in too much Aperol, which makes it syrupy. Aperol gets its flavor from oranges and is part of the amari family, but differs from most in being both low in alcohol (11%) and bitterness. It's essentially Campari for people who don't like Campari and as such does rather get it in the neck from drinks nerds, for whom Campari is the greatest drink in the world (which, let's face it, it probably is.) Still, I love an Aperol Spritz and it is the most adaptable of cocktails.

If you use still wine rather than sparkling, it's called a Bicyclette—it's a great way of using up dull white wine or rosé. It's also delicious with orange, grapefruit, and lemon juice added in place of wine to create a great, very low alcohol drink. You can replace the Aperol with Campari or even, as I sometimes do, go half and half for something with a bit of bite.

---

1 fl oz (30ml) Aperol
2½ fl oz (75ml) Prosecco
¾ fl oz (20ml) fizzy water

Pour the Aperol over ice in a tumbler, add the Prosecco, stir, top up with fizzy water, and stir again. *Garnish with one of those bright green Puglian olives.*

Leave the stirrer in and ideally some fizzy water on the side so you can dilute it if it gets syrupy towards the end.

STUART BALE *from Crucible, London*

Buckfast Tonic Wine is made by monks in Devon, but has proved popular with certain undesirable elements in Scotland. The combination of 15% alcohol and bags of caffeine is supposed to have monstrous effects when drunk to excess. You might think it tastes like the saliva of Satan, but it's actually rather nice, rather like a cough medicine crossed with sweet vermouth with a lick of vanilla at the end.

Noting its similarity to sweet vermouth, it was only logical for Glaswegian bartender Stuart Bale to use Buckfast in a Negroni. Stuart trained as a dentist, but the lure of cocktails was too strong. He worked in bars in Scotland before coming down to London in 2008 and doing a stint at Tony Conigliaro's 69 Colebrooke Row. He now runs the Crucible, not a bar but a sort of mad scientist's laboratory for bartenders, where they can hone their skills with high-tech equipment.

It's a bit sweeter than a standard Negroni and there's also loads of caffeine, so if it does strange things to you, blame the Buckie!

Buckie Negroni

35ml (1¼ fl oz) Campari
35ml (1¼ fl oz) gin
35ml (1¼ fl oz) Buckfast Tonic Wine

Stir with lots of ice in a tumbler, and *serve with a piece of orange zest.*

PICK-ME-UPS

BLOODY MARY

For some reason the Bloody Mary is a drink that is associated with hangovers more than any other. At brunches they serve huge jugs of the stuff. This one is based on Kingsley Amis's recipe, though Amis didn't advise drinking Bloody Marys when suffering from the night before. He thought it too acidic and spicy on a delicate stomach, and who am I to argue with the poet laureate of the hangover? The Bloody Mary certainly doesn't make a particularly good aperitif, or indeed digestif, and it's too heavy for a summer's day sipper. It's more of a meal than a cocktail. Perhaps it really is the ultimate mid-morning drink instead of breakfast, just not on too delicate a stomach.

The addition of a teaspoon of fino sherry is the magic ingredient lifting the whole drink. Go easy on the tabasco; it's not meant to taste hot. My older brother makes them so that they burn your mouth, fun for one sip, but I've never finished one. The ketchup gives it a nice sweet edge. You can buy ready-spiced juices from companies such as Big Tom, but you will still need to tinker with them to get the taste just right for you. Making a good Bloody Mary is like making a good gravy: keep tasting and adjusting until it's perfect for you.

2 fl oz (60ml) vodka
3½ fl oz (100ml) tomato juice
1 tsp tomato ketchup
1 tsp fino sherry
1 tsp lemon juice
dash of Worcestershire sauce
dash of Tabasco
pinch of celery salt
grind of black pepper

Mix the vodka, tomato juice, and a dash of all the other ingredients in a tall glass with ice. Taste, then add more of each until you have it just how you want it. *Garnish with a stick of celery.*

ESPRESSO MARTINI

Another Dick Bradsell creation, invented at the Soho Brasserie in 1983, apparently for a supermodel who wanted something that would wake her up and get her hammered. He christened it the Pharmaceutical Stimulant, but it quickly became known as the Espresso Martini because of the shape of the glass. Despite being a recent invention, it's a cocktail that has inspired much debate as to the proper way to make it. The problem is that it proved so popular that soon bars began cutting corners, even pre-making the whole thing and then just shaking them to order. You must use as good a coffee as you can find, freshly brewed, ideally in a proper espresso machine or in a stovetop moka. This should give you a lovely crema on the top of your cocktail. Add the chilled vodka first and use lots of ice, or you might end up with a coffee slushie.

You can use sugar syrup to sweeten it or leave out the Kahlua altogether so that it's just espresso, vodka, and sugar. If you're feeling really fancy you could use PX sherry for sweetening. Another variation that works quite well is to combine it with the classic Italian drink, the caffè corretto, an espresso with Sambuca on the side, so add a teaspoon of Sambuca for a slight aniseed taste.

1 fl oz (30ml) fresh espresso
1 fl oz (30ml) ice-cold vodka
1 fl oz (30ml) Kahlua

First make a cup of espresso. Add lots of ice to a shaker, then add the vodka and kahlua, stir, and then add the hot coffee. Shake hard and strain into a chilled Martini glass. *Garnish with three coffee beans.* Guaranteed to perk you up.

CORPSE REVIVER NO. 1

There are many drinks purported to cure hangovers. In P.G. Wodehouse's *The Inimitable Jeeves* (1923), Bertie Wooster's butler comes up with a concoction consisting of a raw egg, Worcestershire sauce, and red pepper. Jeeves describes it as "extremely invigorating after a late evening." It's what Americans would call a Prairie Oyster, and the idea is, I think, that it's so unpleasant that it distracts from the pain in the head. Bertie describes it as like "a bomb inside the old bean."

Working on a similar principle is the hangover cure recommended by Fergus Henderson from St John restaurant in London consisting of two parts Fernet Branca to one part Crème de Menthe, drunk over ice. Which sounds like the kind of thing that will send you to an early grave.

The Corpse Reviver is an altogether more generous pick-me-up. It dates back to the 19th century, when there were a whole variety of cocktails designed to get your day off to flying start, such as Gloom Lifters, Eye Openers, Smashers and Morning Jolts. There's also a Corpse Reviver No. 2 for when the No. 1 doesn't work, which consists of gin, triple sec, sweet white vermouth, lemon juice and just a hint of absinthe. If this fails then go back to bed. Here's the No. 1.

1½ fl oz (40ml) brandy
¾ fl oz (20ml) calvados
¾ fl oz (20ml) Italian vermouth

Stir with lots of ice in a shaker and strain into a chilled Martini glass. Drink and, to paraphrase Bertie Wooster, hope will dawn once more.

Overleaf, left to right: Corpse Reviver No. 1, Espresso Martini, Bloody Mary.

HOT DRINKS

MULLED CIDER

I am much more of mulled cider than a mulled wine person. This is because most mulled wine is made badly, whereas if someone is serving you a mulled cider it is usually a sign that they have put some thought into it. Play with the recipe, because sweetness and booze levels vary among ciders. The butter sounds a bit odd, but it gives the cider a lovely creamy quality. The rum or bourbon is optional, but either makes a great addition on a freezing cold December night.

If this is all a bit too much work, you can make an instant hot cider drink by mixing hot cider or even apple juice with ginger liqueur/wine. Use good quality cider, not the stuff made from concentrate—Old Rosie is good. With apple juice use the cloudy stuff that really tastes of apples. My parents have apple trees and they juice the apples that are not used for pies. Every year I say I'm going to make cider out of it, but probably never will.

6 pints (3 liters) good-quality cloudy cider
juice of 3 lemons
juice of 3 oranges
1 tbsp orange zest
½ tbsp lemon zest
1 tbsp sugar
6 cloves
1 cinnamon stick
1 knob of butter
aged rum or bourbon, to taste

Put all the ingredients except the spirits and the butter in a large saucepan. Simmer gently for 30 minutes. Do not boil. Taste; it might need some more sugar. Leave to infuse for as long as you can. Gently reheat. Add the butter, and some bourbon or rum if you want to give it some fire.

MULLED WINE

Mulled wine is a fun, convivial drink and a great way to cater for lots of people on a cold night, but I am sure you, like me, have had some diabolical concoctions calling themselves mulled wine. Problems include using a very, very cheap base wine, boiling it so that all the alcohol comes off, cooking it too long so that the spices go bitter, too much sugar, too little sugar. But it's not a tricky one to get right. Just take a bit of care. Don't skimp on the ingredients. You're aiming for Dickensian generosity, not Scrooge-like parsimony.

The wine is crucial. Don't use anything you wouldn't drink on its own. Avoid painfully thin reds, but don't use anything oaky, as that vanilla taste might spoil the whole thing. I recommend using supermarket Garnacha from Spain, which tends to be full and fruity without being sweet and oaky.

4 bottles of Garnacha or similar
2 cinnamon sticks
3 star anise
2 large pieces of lemon peel (skin only, no pith)
2 large pieces of orange peel (skin only, no pith)
5 cloves
8 tbsp sugar
grating of nutmeg

Cook on a low heat for 15 minutes—do not boil. Take off the heat and leave to infuse. Reheat when your guests come over. Taste; it might need more sugar. If it's too sweet, add some lemon juice and if it starts to taste bitter, fish out the spices.

It's a good idea to keep some rum, port, sloe gin, or brandy in reserve to perk up the mulled wine. In fact, why not discard the mulled wine and just drink the port?

SYRUPS AND FLAVORINGS

Simple sugar syrup

Sugar syrup is endlessly adaptable. You could add rosewater, orange, lime, or lemon juice while you are making it, or leave a piece of lemon peel, vanilla, or a clove in the syrup to slowly infuse.

The ratio is two parts sugar to one part water. Add the water to a pan, heat gently and slowly stir in the sugar. Decant into a sterilized jar (heated in the oven or with boiling water). It will keep for three months in the refrigerator. For a richer flavor use brown sugar.

MINT SYRUP
Make the syrup as above but add a handful of fresh cleaned mint. Leave to steep for an hour or so and then strain into a sterilized jar. Use to make the perfect Mint Julep or Mojito.

SMOKED WAKAME SUGAR SYRUP
Make the syrup as above but add a strip of wakame (see page 222). Leave to steep for an hour or so and then strain into a sterilized jar.

Grenadine

Grenadine is French for pomegranate, but many brands of grenadine contain no pomegranate. They are essentially just colored and flavored syrups. Making your own is easy. All you need is pomegranate juice—pure pomegranate juice, not a drink containing pomegranate—and sugar.

Aove, left to right: Bramble liqueur, mint sugar syrup, raspberry shrub.

Make it much like making a simple syrup. Pomegranate juice is already sweet so you don't need to add as much sugar. A ratio of two parts juice to three parts sugar works well. Pour the pomegranate juice in a saucepan and gently heat—don't boil. Add the sugar slowly and stir until it dissolves. Remove from the heat, pour into a sterilized jar and it should last in the refrigerator for months.

Raspberry shrub

Shrubs are flavored sweetened vinegars, but taste a lot better than they sound. These were very popular in 17th and 18th-century Britain and

America, but disappeared in the 20th century. You can use them in fruity cocktails and they work well just mixed with a little soda water or ginger ale. Here's a recipe for a very basic raspberry shrub. You could make something similar by cooking fruit in a basic syrup, straining, and then adding vinegar. You can use any fruit and you can play about with honey, herbs, spices, and different types of vinegar.

7 oz (200g) raspberries
5 oz (150g) granulated sugar
7 fl oz (200ml) good-quality fruit vinegar

Mash the raspberries and sugar together and leave overnight to steep. The sugar should dissolve in the raspberry juice. The next day push the mixture through a fine sieve, keep the sweet juice, and discard the solids. Mix the raspberry juice with vinegar. Pour into a sterilized jar. Store in the refrigerator for up to 3 months.

Crème de Mûre (blackberry liqueur)

Crème de Mûre is simply the blackberry version of Crème de Cassis (blackcurrant liqueur). It isn't tricky to make your own. Late summer and early autumn is a good time to start making your own drinks. Sloes are the most common fruit to make into a drink, but last year we had a glut of brambles, or balckberries. It seemed like every hedge, wood, or patch of waste ground in London was teeming with fruit. So I decided to make bramble liqueur. Don't worry too much about the quality of the spirit. You don't really want anything with too much flavor. I used a mixture of gin and vodka. You can make versions of this by using raspberries, blackcurrants, or strawberries as your base. Just remember to garnish with the right fruit.

1 lb (500g) blackberries
1 lb (500g) granulated sugar
3 pints (1.5 liters) gin and/or vodka
juice of 1 lemon
bay leaf

Wash the blackberries and remove any sad-looking ones, caterpillars, and bits of leaf. Sterilize a large resealable jar by washing it and then pouring boiling water over it. Put all the ingredients in the jar. Shake the jar vigorously and put in a cool dark place. Keep it there for 3 months and shake once a week. After 3 months it's time to decant it. You can steep for up to 6 months but no longer as the blackberries will impart a woody flavor. Strain the liquid and decant into sterilizsed bottles, jars etc.

Bacon bourbon

The Cocktail Book from 1900 has recipes for all different kinds of Old Fashioneds made with English gin, Dutch gin, or brandy, but I think the ultimate one is made with bacon-infused bourbon.

¾ pint (400ml) bourbon
4 slices of smoked streaky bacon

Cook the bacon in a pan so that it goes crispy and all the fat has rendered out. Eat the bacon. Pour the bacon fat and bourbon into a glass jar, put the lid on, shake, and then leave to infuse overnight. Put the jar in the freezer for a few hours so that the fat solidifies. Remove the fat from the bourbon and strain the bacon-infused spirit through muslin. You are now ready to make a bacon Old Fashioned (see page 218).

Simple orange bitters

You will need strong alcohol to make bitters. In Italy they have plastic containers of almost pure alcohol available in every supermarket for making your own limoncello or amaro. In America you can buy Everclear at 95%, but in Britain such pure alcohol is hard to find and very expensive because of the high level of duty. Weaker alcohol will mean a longer steeping time. Rob Berry from Asterley Bros, which makes amari and bitters in a garage in south London, told me that the harder the spice, the longer it will need in alcohol. Milk thistle, gentian, and burdock roots all require lots of time to release flavors. Orange peel gives up its flavor much more easily. Rob uses whole spices, but he says that if you can't get hold of high-strength alcohol you might want grind your ingredients. He also steeps his ingredients separately and then blends them, but you probably won't have the space or patience to do this at home. With bitters you are looking more for flavor than refinement.

This is a very basic orange bitters recipe. Ingredients are approximate—if in doubt err on the side of too much. You want to extract as much flavor as you can. You could sweeten with ordinary white sugar, but brown sugar gives it nice color and weight.

Opposite: Making your own orange bitters is relatively easy, though you will need to shake it every day to get the best flavor.

1 pint (500ml) grain alcohol
1 pint (500ml) water
peel of 2 oranges, dried and chopped (no pith)
peel of 1 grapefruit dried and chopped (ditto)
1 tsp anise seeds or 1 star anise
2 cloves
1 cinnamon stick, crushed
4 cardamom pods, crushed
2 tsp coriander seeds, crushed
3½ oz (100g) brown sugar, to taste

In a large jar steep everything except the sugar in the alcohol for about a month. The higher the strength of the alchol, the less time you need. Shake it every day and after a month taste it. If it's not strongly flavored then it needs longer.

After a month (or more depending on the strength of the alcohol) finely strain the alcohol through a muslin and reserve in a jar. Take the ingredients that were in the alcohol and put in a saucepan, cover with water, and simmer for 10 minutes, then pour the water with the fruit and spices into a jar. Leave for a week, shaking every day. Strain through a muslin, keep the flavored water, and discard the rest.

This flavored water is for diluting the bitters to a drinkable strength. In a resealable jar add half the flavored water to the alcohol, and taste. If it blows your head off, add more flavored water. You want it to be intense, but not overpowering. When you are happy, add some brown sugar gradually. Keep tasting: you want the sugar to balance the bitterness without overpowering it. When you are happy, seal, shake, and keep for a week to meld.

GARNISHES

The big four garnishes are the maraschino cherry, the olive, a sprig of mint or something involving citrus fruit.

The purpose of a twist or piece of peel isn't just to look nice, but because in making the twist you express some of the oils from the skin of the fruit into the drink, which is why you should buy unwaxed fruit and wash it. Some drinks will call for the oil then for the twist to be discarded.

You can simply take off some peel with a sharp fruit peeler (avoiding the bitter pith), twist it over the drink just before serving, and drop it in.

To make something a little fancier, take your lemon (or lime or orange), cut both ends off, then very carefully put a small knife or barspoon between the pulp and rind and saw around the fruit so that you separate the juicy bit from the skin. You need to do this carefully so that you have no pulp attached to the skin. Then slice along the skin lengthways and pop the insides out. You will be left with a big piece of skin casing. Roll this tightly like a very small carpet and cut it into thin sections along the perpendicular. These will be your twists. When your drink is ready, take a section of skin, roll it up tight, and then pull it over the drink—this will release the oils. It should then spring into a twist shape and you can drop it into the drink.

Below, left to right: Garnishes in a Mojito, Martini, and Old Fashioned.

FURTHER EXPLORATION

BOOKS

Anon: *The Cocktail Book*, London 1900

Amis, Kingsley: *Everyday Drinking*, London 2008

Barr, Andrew: *A Social History*, London 1995

Benton, Charlotte & Tim: *Art Deco 1910–39*, London 2015

Jessica Boak and Ray Bailey: *20th Century Pub*, London 2017

Craddock, Harry: *Savoy Cocktail Book*, London 1930

De Voto, Bernard: *The Hour*, New York 1910

Felton, Eric: *How's your Drink?*, New York 2007

Fiell, Charlotte & Peter: *Decorative Arts 50s*, Cologne 2008

Forsyth, Mark: *A Short History of Drunkenness*, London 2017

Gately, Iain, Drink: *A Cultural History of Alcohol*, London 2008

Godwin, Richard, *The Spirits*, London 2015

Jeffreys, Henry: *Empire of Booze: British History through the Bottom of a Glass*, London 2016

Miller, Judith: *Mid-Century Modern: Living with Mid-Century Modern Design*, London 2012

Moore, Victoria: *How to Drink*, London 2010

WEBSITES

Punch Drunk
https://punchdrink.com

Difford's Guide
www.diffordsguide.com/

Modern Drunkard
https://drunkard.com

Tiki with Ray
www.tikiwithray.com/

DRINK

Gerry's
Old Compton Street, Soho
London W1D 4UW
www.gerrys.uk.com

The Whisky Exchange
2 Bedford St, Covent Garden
London WC2E 9HH
www.thewhiskyexchange.com

Master of Malt
www.masterofmalt.com

Gordon & MacPhail
58–60 South Street
Elgin IV30 1JY
www.gordonandmacphail.com

Ambassador Wines and Spirits
1020 2nd Avenue
New York, NY 10022
ambassadorwines.com

Park Avenue Liquor Shop
292 Madison Avenue
New York, NY 10017
www.parkaveliquor.com

Hi Times
250 Ogle St., Costa Mesa
Los Angeles, CA 92627
www.hitimewine.net

Bar Keeper
3910 Sunset Blvd, Silver Lake
Los Angeles, CA 90029
www.barkeepersilverlake.com

Vendome
270 S Robertson Blvd,
Beverly Hills, CA 90211
and branches around LA
www.vendometolucalake.com/

P&V Wine and Liquor Merchants
64 Enmore Road, Newtown
Sydney, NSW 2042
www.pnvmerchants.com

BAR MANUFACTURERS

Quench Homes Bars
Studio 29, Woodham Waye
Woking, Surrey GU21 5SJ
www.quenchhomebars.com

John Cowell
PO Box 1319,
Preston, PR2 0RX
www.john-cowell.com/

Copper and Zinc Bar Company
Unit C, Riverside Business Studios
Bendon Valley,
London SW18 4UQ
thecopperandzincbarco.com

Home Bars USA
www.homebarsusa.com

Atlanta Custom Bars
5020 S Atlanta Rd SE #5
Atlanta, GA 30339
www.classicbars.net

Tiki Bar Central
www.tikibarcentral.com

Home Bars, Australia
https://homebars.com.au

BAR AND KITCHEN EQUIPMENT

Cocktail Kingdom
www.cocktailkingdom.co.uk

Waiter's Friend
http://waitersfriend.co.uk

London Bar and Kitchen
www.londonbarandkitchen.com

Lakeland Plastic
www.lakeland.co.uk

Cream Supplies
www.creamsupplies.co.uk

John Lewis
branches around country
www.johnlewis.com

Nesbits Catering Equipment
www.nisbets.co.uk

Oliver Bonas
shops around country
www.oliverbonas.com

Bar Products
www.barproducts.com

Bar Supplies
https://barsupplies.com

Sur La Table
branches around country
www.surlatable.com

Williams Sonoma
shops around the country
www.williams-sonoma.com

GLASSWARE
The Riedel Shop
www.theriedelshop.co.uk

Dartington
www.dartington.co.uk

Zalto
www.zalto.co.uk

UNUSUAL INGREDIENTS
Holland & Barrett
www.hollandandbarrett.com

Healthy Supplies
www.healthysupplies.co.uk

American Spice
www.americanspice.com/

BRIC A BRAC AND RETRO
Aladdin's Cave
72 Loampit Hill
London SE13 7SX
+44 020 8320 2553

Bambino
32 Church Rd
London SE19 2ET
+44 07956 323164

Crystal Palace Antiques,
Imperial House, Jasper Rd
London SE19 1SG
+44 020 8480 7042

The Old Cinema
160 Chiswick High Road
London W4 1PR
www.theoldcinema.co.uk

Vintage Thrift Shop
286 3rd Ave
New York, NY 10010
+1 212-871-0777

Furnish Green
1261 Broadway #309
New York, NY 10001
http://furnishgreen.com

Helping Hand Thrift Shop
4402, 1033 S Fairfax Ave
Los Angeles, CA 90019
+1 323-857-1191

Sydney Used Furniture
500 Marrickville Rd, Dulwich Hill
NSW 2203, Australia
+61 2 9560 1444

VAMPT Vintage Design
486/490 Elizabeth St
Surry Hills, NSW 2010
https://vamptvintagedesign.com

Great Dane
613 Elizabeth Street
Redfern, NSW 2016
https://greatdanefurniture.com

NEW FURNITURE
Houzz has websites in the UK, US
and Australia: https://www.houzz.
com/

Skandium
86 Marylebone High St
London W1U 4QS
www.skandium.com

Peppermill Interiors
Unit 6, Ring Road, Zone 2
Burntwood Business Park
Burntwood, London WS7 3JQ
www.peppermillinteriors.com

Cult Furniture
www.cultfurniture.com

Chaplins
https://chaplins.co.uk

Modernlink
35 Bond St,
New York, NY 10012
www.modernlink.com

Restoration Hardware
www.restorationhardware.com

Pottery Barn
www.potterybarn.com

IQMatics European Furniture
Bauer Building, 230 W Huron St,
Chicago, IL 60654

Barney's New York,
www.barneys.com

Furniture Melbourne
352 Boundary Road,
Dingley Village
Melbourne VIC 3172
https://modernfurniture.com.au

Macleay On Manning
1/85 Macleay Street, Potts Point
Sydney, NSW 2011
https://macleayonmanning

POSTERS AND ARTWORK
Spencer Weisz Galleries
Chicago, IL 60610
www.antiqueposters.com

At the Movies
18 Thayer St, Marylebone
London W1U 3JY
www.atthemovies.co.uk/

La Belle Epoque
115 Greenwich Ave,
New York, NY 10014,
www.vintageposters.us

BEER AND DISTILLATION EQUIPMENT
Beer Hawk
www.beerhawk.co.uk

Pub Shop
www.pubshop.co.uk

Love Brewing
www.lovebrewing.co.uk

Kegworks
global.kegworks.com

Micromatic
www.micromatic.com/

Copper Alembic
www.copper-alembic.com/en
Portugal, but ship globally

INDEX

Page numbers in *italics* refer to illustrations

ACKNOWLEDGMENTS

Author's Acknowledgments
I would like to thank the following people for their help in researching this book: Alice Lascelles, Ian Buxton, Victoria Moore, Dr Nick Morgan, Alessandro Palazzi, Stephen Bayley, Stuart Ekins, Sother Teague, Erik Lorincz, Eoin Kenny, Jake Blanch, Stuart Bale, Andy Ferreira, Jim Meehan, Fraser Hamilton, Eamon "el Tigre" Ramos, Charlie Lamont, and Jonathan Green. I would also like to thank Misti Traya, and Dustin and Grace Louw for their tireless work tasting and honing the cocktail recipes.

Publisher's Acknowledgments
Thanks to Alexandre Ricard for providing the foreword and for allowing Simon Upton to photograph his home bar, Jonathan Green of Quench Home Bar, Mark McClintock for mixing cocktails, and Riedel for the loan of glassware for special photography.

PICTURE CREDITS

Page 1 Simon Upton/Interior Archive, designer Haynes Roberts; **2** Douglas Friedman/Interior Archive, designer Eric Hughes; **4** GAP Interiors/House & Leisure/S Chance, designer Debra Parkingson; **7** Simon Upton/Interior Archive, project direction Daniel Gaujac, designer Gaëtan Lebegue; **8** above left Simon Upton/Interior Archive, bar accessories Le Bain Marie; **8** above right Simon Upton/Interior Archive, bar accessories Le Bain Marie; **8** below Simon Upton/Interior Archive, project direction Daniel Gaujac, photograph Eric Morin, vintage shakers Mauro Mahjoub & Fernando Castellon; **10/11** Simon Upton/Interior Archive, project direction Daniel Gaujac, designer Gaëtan Lebegue, table design Stefan Nicolaev; **13** Douglas Friedman/Interior Archive, designer Ken Fulk; **14** Heritage Image Partnership Ltd/Alamy Stock Photo; **17** Mehdi Fedouach/AFP/Getty Images; **18** Frederic Lewis/Archive Photos/Getty Images; **19** Topical Press Agency/Getty Images; **20** SSPL/Getty Images; **22** above R Gates/Frederic Lewis/Archive Photos/Getty Images; **22** below Archive Photos/Getty Images; **23** above Getty Images; **23** below Ullstein Bild via Getty Images; **25** Douglas Friedman/Interior Archive, designer Ken Fulk, de Gournay; **26/27** Douglas Friedman/Interior Archive, designer Ken Fulk; **28** Martinus Andersen/Conde Nast via Getty Images; **30/31** Bettmann/Getty Images, artist Alfred R Thompson; **32** above Randy Duchaine/Alamy Stock Photo; **32** below Matthew Richardson/Alamy Stock Photo, artist Alfred R Thompson; **33** Andy Stagg-VIEW/Alamy Stock Photo; **34** GAP Interiors/John Downs; **35** Peter Cavanagh/Alamy Stock Photo; **36/37** Douglas Friedman/Interior Archive, designer Ken Fulk; **38** Simon Upton/Interior Archive, project direction Daniel Gaujac, designer Vaughan Yates of 1751; **39** Alexander James/Interior Archive, designer Turner Pocock; **41** Eric Nathan/Alamy Stock Photo; **42** Peter Sylvester Photography http://petersylvesterphotography.com/; **43** James Fennell/Interior Archive; **44** Alexander James/Interior Archive, designer Mark Gillette; **45** Joanna Maclennan/Interior Archive; **46/47** Simon Upton/Interior Archive, designer Bibi Monnahan; **48** A Y Owen/The LIFE Images Collection/Getty Images; **49** Simon Upton/Interior Archive, project direction Daniel Gaujac, designer Vaughan Yates of 1751, architect Rafael Gallego, with Patrick Guidici and Eric Fossard; **50** Christopher Simon Sykes/Interior Archive, designer Vivien Leone; **51** above left Sam Mellish/In Pictures via Getty Images; **51** above right Jenny Zarins http://www.jennyzarins.com/; **51** below Douglas Friedman/Interior Archive, designer Marc Meiré; **52/53** luckyraccoon/Shutterstock; **54/55** Anjali Pinto/Lettuce Entertain You Restaurants; **56** Cath Harries/Alamy Stock Photo; **57** Simon Upton/Quarto Books, designer Hubert Zandberg, artist Heim Steinbach; **58/59** Michel Arnaud/Interior Archive, designer India Hicks; **61** Gwengoat/Getty Images; **62/63** Douglas Friedman/Interior Archive, designer Ken Fulk; **64** Douglas Friedman/Interior Archive, designer Martyn Lawrence Bullard, artist Tracey Emin; **65** Fritz von der Schulenburg/Interior Archive, designer Trevor Dykman; **66** above INTERFOTO/Alamy Stock Photo; **66** below GAP Interiors/Costas Picadas, designer Stefano Giovannoni; **67** above Douglas Friedman/Interior Archive, designer Bryan Graybill and Alex Harris; **67** below Douglas Friedman/Interior Archive, designer Ken Fulk; **68/69** Quench Bars, interior designer Penelope Allen Design; **71** above left Eric d'Hérouville/Basset Images; **71** above right GAP Interiors/Costas Picadas; **71** below Hoxton/Alamy Stock Photo; **72** Fritz von der Schulenburg/Interior Archive, designer John Stefanidis; **73** GAP Interiors/Costas Picadas; **74** Mireille Roobaert/Basset Images; **75** Stefano Scata/Interior Archive; **76/77** Michel Arnaud/Interior Archive, architect Allen Bianchi; **78/79** Eric Cuvillier www.ericcuvillier.com; **81** Patrice Hauser/SCOPE-IMAGE/Alamy Stock Photo; **82** Douglas Friedman/Interior Archive, designer Nicole Hollis; **83** Douglas Friedman/Interior Archive, designer Marc Meiré; **84** above left GAP Interiors/Costas Picadas; **84** above right Andrew Wood/Quarto Books, Azman Owens Architects; **84** below Astronaut/Getty Images; **85** Douglas Friedman/Interior Archive, designer Eddie Lee, Mark Hampton; **86** Getty Images; **87** Douglas Friedman/Interior Archive, designer Nicole Holllis; **88/89** Douglas Friedman/Interior Archive, designer Ken Fulk; **90** left Alexander James/Interior Archive; **90** right Simon Upton/Interior Archive, designer Hubert Zandberg; **91** Simon Upton/Interior Archive, designer Nicky Haslam; **92** Simon Upton/Interior Archive, designer Nicky Haslam; **93** above Fritz von der Schulenburg/Interior Archive; **93** below left GAP Interiors/Douglas Gibb; **93** below right GAP Interiors/Ingrid Rasmussen; **94** GAP Interiors/David Giles; **95** Courtesy of Restoration Hardware https://www.restorationhardware.com/; **96** Douglas Friedman/Interior Archive, designers Veronica Swanson Beard, Chiqui Woolworth, Brittany Bromley; **97** Fritz von der Schulenburg/Interior Archive, designer Nicky Haslam; **99** Simon Upton/Quarto Books, designer Hubert Zandberg, artist David Goldblatt; **100** above Simon Upton/Quarto Books, Quench Home Bars; **100** below Simon Upton/Quarto Books, designer Hubert Zandberg, Sergio Rodrigues; **101** above Simon Upton/Quarto Books, designer Nicky Haslam; **101** below Mark Luscombe-Whyte/Interior Archive, designer Hubert Zandberg, artist Gert & Uwe Tobias; **102** Douglas Friedman/Interior Archive, designer Ken Fulk; **103** Fritz von der Schulenburg/Interior Archive, designer Meret Oppenheim; **104** left; Fritz von der Schulenburg/Interior Archive; **104** right Simon Upton/Quarto Books, designer Nicky Haslam; **105** Douglas Friedman/Interior Archive, designer David Jimenez; **106/107** Pavel Losevsky/Alamy Stock Photo; **108** Eric d'Hérouville/Basset Images; **110** Simon Upton/Quarto Books, Quench Home Bars; **112/113** Cath Harries/Alamy Stock Photo; **114** above left Simon Upton/Interior Archive, project direction Daniel Gaujac; **114** above right Andreas von Einseidel, designer Jones Lambell; **114** below GAP Interiors/Colin Poole; **115** Nicolas Matheus/Basset Images; **116** Tim Beddow/Interior Archive, architect Patrick Gwynne; **117** Roman Sigaev/Alamy Stock Photo; **118** GAP Interiors/Costas Picadas, Claire Maestroni, Giorgio Stefano; **119** above SO Visual Ltd for Peppermill Interiors www.peppermillinteriors.com; **119** below Simon Upton/Quarto Books, Quench Home Bars; **120/121** 79Photography/Alamy Stock Photo; **122** Alexander James/Interior Archive, designer Ham Interiors; **123** Simon Upton/Interior Archive, designer Gaëtan Lebegue, project direction Daniel Gaujac; **124** Douglas Friedman/Interior Archive, designer Ken Fulk; **125** Luke White/Interior Archive, designer Hubert Zandberg; **126** Douglas Friedman/Interior Archive, designer Ken Fulk; **127** Andreas von Einseidel, designer Candy & Candy; **128/129** Douglas Friedman/Interior Archive, designer Ken Fulk; **130** above left Luke White/Interior Archive, designer Hubert Zandberg; **130** above right William Waldron/Interior Archive, designer Frank Muytjens; **130** below left Jean-Marc Palisse/Cote Paris, designer Caroline Sarkozy; **130** below right Fritz von der Schulenburg/Interior Archive, designer Stephen Mayers; **131** above left GAP Interiors/Costas Picadas; **131** below left Andreas von Einseidel, designer Kate Murphy; **131** right Andreas von Einseidel; **132** Andrew Twort/Interior Archive, designer Candy & Candy; **133** Douglas Friedman/Interior Archive, designer Ken Fulk; **134/135** Courtesy of Restoration Hardware https://www.restorationhardware.com/; **136** left Simon Upton/Interior Archive, project direction Daniel Gaujac, mixologist Sasha Molodskikh; **136** right Simon Upton/Interior Archive, project direction Daniel Gaujac, mixologist Sasha Molodskikh; **137** Simon Upton/Interior Archive, project direction Daniel Gaujac, mixologist Sasha Molodskikh; **138** Simon Upton/Interior Archive, project direction Daniel Gaujac, mixologist Sasha Molodskikh; **139** Simon Upton/Quarto Books, Quench Home Bars; **140/141** Alexander James/Interior Archive, designer Ham Interiors; **142** Quench Home Bars; **143** Simon Smith/Quarto Books; **144** Eric Travers/Gamma-Rapho/Getty Images; **145** Simon Upton/Interior Archive, project direction Daniel Gaujac, designer Mathieu Mercier, vintage shakers Mauro Mahjoub & Fernando Castellon; **146** Simon Upton/Interior Archive, project direction Daniel Gaujac, mixologist Sasha Molodskikh, vintage shakers Mauro Mahjoub & Fernando Castellon; **147** Simon Upton/Interior Archive, project direction Daniel Gaujac, mixologist Sasha Molodskikh; **148** above left Simon Upton/Interior Archive; **148** above right; Luke White/Interior Archive, designer Hubert Zandberg; **148** below migstock/Alamy Stock Photo; **149** The Old Cinema www.theoldcinema.co.uk Shutterstock; **150** Simon Smith/Quarto Books; **151** Simon Smith/Quarto Books; **152** Richard Jung/Quarto Books; **154** left and right; Simon Upton/Quarto Books, Quench Home Bars; **155** Simon Upton/Interior Archive; **156** Kevin Summers/Quarto Books; **157** Richard Jung/Quarto Books; **158** above left James Fennell/Interior Archive; **158** above right Nicolas Tosi/Coté Ouest; **158** below Luke White/Interior Archive; **159** above left George Oze/Alamy Stock Photo; **159** below left Simon Upton/Interior Archive, project direction Daniel Gaujac, mixologist Sasha Molodskikh; **159** right Jean-Marc Palisse/Coté Paris, designer Hiroyuki Tsugawa; **161** Museum of the City of New York/Gottscho-Schleisner/Getty Images; **162/163** Simon Smith/Quarto Books; **164** Simon Smith/Quarto Books; **165** Simon Smith/Quarto Books; **167** Simon Upton/Quarto Books, Quench Home Bars; **168** Simon Upton/Interior Archive, project direction Daniel Gaujac, mixologist Sasha Molodskikh; **171** Arunas Gabalis/Alamy Stock Photo; **172/173** Christoph Lischetzki/Alamy Stock Photo; **174** GAP Interiors/House & Leisure, Elsa Young, Stylist Leana Schoeman; **176** Simon Upton/Quarto Books, Quench Home Bars; **177** Simon Upton/Quarto Books, Quench Home Bars; **178** Simon Upton/Quarto Books, Quench Home Bars; **180** Simon Upton/Quarto Books, Quench Home Bars; **183** Kim Lightbody/Quarto Books; **184** Simon Smith/Quarto Books; **185** Richard Jung/Quarto Books; **186** Simon Upton/Quarto Books, Quench Home Bars; **188/189** Simon Upton/Interior Archive, designer Gaëtan Lebegue, project direction Daniel Gaujac; **191** travelb europe/Alamy Stock Photo; **192** Ed Anderson; **194** Quarto Books; **197** Simon Smith/Quarto Books; **199** Simon Murrell/Quarto Books; **201** John Carey/Quarto Books; **203** Simon Smith/Quarto Books **204/205** luckyraccoon/Shutterstock; **206** Getty Images; **207–250** Simon Smith/Quarto Books.